Welcome Home
30-MINUTE
COOKBOOK

QUICK & EASY EVERYDAY MEALS

Hope Comerford
Photos by Bonnie Matthews

10 9 8 7 6 5 4 3 2 1

Names: Comerford, Hope, author. | Matthews, Bonnie, 1963- photographer.
Title: Welcome home 30-minute cookbook : quick & easy everyday meals / Hope
    Comerford ; photos by Bonnie Matthews.
Description: New York, New York : Good Books, [2023] | Series: Fix-it and
    forget-it | Includes index. | Summary: "127 recipes for stovetop, oven,
    Instant Pot, and slow cooker"-- Provided by publisher.
Identifiers: LCCN 2023001174 (print) | LCCN 2023001175 (ebook) | ISBN
    9781680998641 (paperback) | ISBN 9781680998801 (epub)
Subjects: LCSH: Quick and easy cooking. | LCGFT: Cookbooks.
Classification: LCC TX833.5 .C646 2023 (print) | LCC TX833.5 (ebook) |
    DDC 641.5/12--dc23/eng/20230127
LC record available at https://lccn.loc.gov/2023001174
LC ebook record available at https://lccn.loc.gov/2023001175

Cover design by David Ter-Avanesyan
Cover photos by Bonnie Matthews

Print ISBN: 978-1-68099-864-1
Ebook ISBN: 978-1-68099-880-1

Printed in China

Table of Contents

About Welcome Home 30-Minute Cookbook

If you're like me, you have no time to spare, especially when it comes to getting a meal on the table each night. I've got 127 amazing recipes to choose from, all of which take 30 minutes or less from prep to table. Whether you're looking for breakfast for dinner, a new salad to try, a hearty chili or soup, or even something to throw on the grill, you'll find it all right here. I've included recipes for things like Oven French Toast, Ginger Chicken Noodle Soup, Meatball Tortellini Soup, Barbecue Chicken Pizza, Lemon Grilled Chicken Breasts, Shrimp Primavera, BLT Pasta Salad, and *so* much more!

As you begin your journey through this book, bear in mind that I always suggest reading it from cover to cover. I can't tell you the good recipes I've missed in the past by not following this advice. Bookmark or dog-ear the pages of the recipes that your family would enjoy the most, or that fit with their dietary needs. Then, when you've looked at everything, go back to those marked pages and narrow your selection down. Make yourself a grocery list and grab what you don't already have. Voilà! You're ready to get cooking! I can't wait for you to discover your favorite quick and easy recipes!

Greek Eggs

Rosanne Hankins, Stevensville, MD

Makes 4 servings

Prep. Time: 5 minutes   *Cooking Time: 12–15 minutes*

2 cloves garlic, sliced
¼ cup sliced white onion
1 Tbsp. oil
1 lb. fresh chopped spinach
8 eggs, beaten
1 Tbsp. fresh chopped oregano
4 oz. feta cheese

1. In large skillet, sauté garlic and onion in oil for 3–4 minutes.

2. Stir in spinach and let wilt.

3. Pour eggs and oregano into hot skillet.

4. Cook, turning 2–3 times, until eggs are lightly cooked, about 5 minutes.

5. Turn off heat; crumble cheese over top of spinach-egg mixture. Cover and let set for 2 minutes, or until cheese melts into eggs.

Variations:

1. For added color and flavor, stir half a sweet red bell pepper, chopped, into Step 1.

2. For additional flavor, add ¼ tsp. black or white pepper and ⅛ tsp. salt in Step 3.

Delicious Shirred Eggs

Hope Comerford, Clinton Township, MI

Makes 6 servings

Prep. Time: 5 minutes ⚶ *Cooking Time: 2–3 minutes*

2 Tbsp. fresh minced onion

1 clove garlic, minced

6 Tbsp. skim milk, *divided*

6 jumbo eggs

6 Tbsp. fresh Parmesan cheese, grated, *divided*

Fresh cracked pepper

1 cup water

1. Spray 6 ramekins with nonstick cooking spray.

2. Evenly divide the minced onion and garlic between the 6 ramekins.

3. Pour 1 Tbsp. of milk into each ramekin.

4. Break an egg into each ramekin.

5. Top each egg with 1 Tbsp. freshly grated cheese.

6. Season with fresh cracked pepper.

7. Pour the water into the bottom of the Instant Pot. Place the trivet on top.

8. Arrange 3 ramekins on top of the trivet, then carefully stack the remaining 3 ramekins on top, staggering their positions so each ramekin on top is sitting between 2 on the bottom layer.

9. Secure the lid and set the vent to sealing.

10. Set the Instant Pot to low pressure and manually set the cook time to 2 minutes for runny yolks or 3 minutes for hard yolks.

11. When the cook time is over, manually release the pressure and remove the lid. Serve immediately.

Elegant Scrambled Eggs

John D. Allen, Rye, CO

Makes 6–8 servings

Prep. Time: 15 minutes   Cooking Time: 10 minutes

12 eggs

½ tsp. salt

⅛ tsp. pepper

2 Tbsp. butter

2 Tbsp. whipping cream

1. Combine the first three ingredients in a large bowl. Beat until well mixed.

2. Melt butter in a skillet, making sure the bottom is covered. Add eggs. Set the heat at medium.

3. Stir constantly until eggs firm up but are not dry. Remove from heat.

4. Stir in the cream. Serve immediately.

Old-Timey French Toast

Jennifer Kellogg, Whately, MA

Makes 4–6 servings

Prep. Time: 5 minutes   *Cooking Time: 5–8 minutes*

1 cup milk

2 whole eggs

¼ cup sugar

1 tsp. grated nutmeg, *divided*

16-oz. loaf of sliced bread, white or wheat

1. In a large mixing bowl, whisk together the milk, eggs, sugar, and half of the nutmeg.

2. Spray bottom of skillet with cooking spray.

3. Dip individual slices of bread into milk mixture and place in hot skillet. Cook until golden brown.

4. Sprinkle each slice with remaining nutmeg. Flip over to brown the other side.

5. Serve immediately.

Oven French Toast

Rhoda Nissley, Parkesburg, PA

Makes 6–8 servings

Prep. Time: 10 minutes   Cooking Time: 15 minutes

1 cup orange juice

6 beaten eggs

¼ tsp. ground cardamom, *optional*

1 stick (½ cup) butter

12 slices sturdy white bread

½–1 cup maple syrup, warmed

1. Preheat oven to 450°F.

2. In a shallow bowl, combine orange juice and eggs. Blend well.

3. Add cardamom if you wish.

4. Divide butter between two 10 × 15-inch jelly roll pans.

5. Place pans in oven to melt butter. Remove from oven when butter is melted.

6. One by one, dip bread slices in egg mixture to coat both sides. Place 6 slices on each pan.

7. Bake at 450°F for 5 minutes. Turn each slice over and bake 5 more minutes.

8. Drizzle with syrup before serving.

Strawberry Pancakes

Becky Frey, Lebanon, PA

Makes 15 medium-sized pancakes, or 4–5 servings

Prep. Time: 10–15 minutes   Cooking Time: 10 minutes

2 eggs

1 cup buttermilk

1 cup crushed strawberries*

¼ cup oil

1 tsp. almond extract

2 cups whole wheat (or white) flour

2 Tbsp. brown sugar

2 tsp. baking powder

1 tsp. baking soda

1. In large mixing bowl beat eggs until fluffy.

2. Stir buttermilk, strawberries, oil, and almond extract into eggs.

3. In a separate bowl, combine flour, brown sugar, baking powder, and baking soda. Add to wet ingredients. Beat together with whisk just until smooth.

4. Heat skillet or griddle until a few drops of water sizzle when sprinkled on top. Fry pancakes until bubbly on top. Flip and continue cooking until browned. Strawberries can scorch, so keep checking to make sure they're not burning. Turn the heat lower if necessary.

* You can use fresh or frozen berries. If frozen, thaw them and drain them well before mixing into batter.

Serving suggestion:

Top finished pancakes with vanilla yogurt and fruit sauce and serve for breakfast, brunch, a light lunch, or supper, or as a dessert.

Berry-Topped Wheat Pancakes

STOVETOP

Anne Nolt, Thompsontown, PA

Makes 6 servings

Prep. Time: 10 minutes ⚜ *Cooking Time: 15–20 minutes*

1 cup whole wheat pastry flour

½ cup wheat germ

1 Tbsp. sugar

2 tsp. baking powder

¼ tsp. baking soda

¾ cup orange juice

¾ cup plain yogurt

2 Tbsp. canola oil

1 large egg, or 2 egg whites

2 cups blueberries

Blueberry Sauce:

¼ cup sugar

2 Tbsp. cornstarch

1 cup water

4 cups blueberries

1. In medium bowl, combine dry ingredients. Mix well.

2. In small bowl, combine orange juice, yogurt, oil, and egg. Blend well.

3. Add liquid ingredients to dry ingredients.

4. Add 2 cups blueberries.

5. Stir everything together gently, just until dry ingredients are moistened.

6. Pour batter by ¼ cupfuls onto hot, lightly greased griddle or into large skillet.

7. Turn when bubbles form on top.

8. Cook until second side is golden brown. Continue this process until all the batter is cooked.

9. Meanwhile, make the blueberry sauce. In a medium saucepan combine sugar and cornstarch. Gradually stir in water. Add the blueberries.

10. Bring to a boil over medium heat, and let boil for 2 minutes, stirring constantly.

11. Remove from the heat. Serve with pancakes.

Apple Cinnamon Pan Biscuits

Gretchen Maust, Keezletown, VA

Makes 20 servings

Prep. Time: 10 minutes ⚮ *Cooking Time: 15–20 minutes*

3½ cups self-rising flour
½ tsp. cinnamon
⅔ cup shortening
I large apple
1¼ cups milk

1. In a mixing bowl, stir the flour and cinnamon to combine. Cut in the shortening with a pastry cutter until thoroughly mixed.

2. Grate the apple and stir it gently into mixture.

3. Add the milk and mix lightly. Too much stirring will cause the biscuits to be tough.

4. Pat the dough into a greased jelly-roll pan. Bake at 400°F just until lightly browned.

5. Add Topping (recipe below) if you wish. Cut into squares and serve warm.

Optional Topping

When the biscuits finish baking, drizzle with a glaze made by mixing 2 Tbsp. melted butter, 3 Tbsp. milk, 1½ cups confectioners' sugar, and ½ tsp. cinnamon together or sprinkle with confectioners' sugar.

Spinach and Mushroom Frittata

J. B. Miller, Indianapolis, IN

Makes 4 servings

Prep. Time: 5 minutes ❧ *Cooking Time: 10 minutes*

6 eggs

½ tsp. salt

¼ tsp. black pepper

1 Tbsp. minced fresh basil

3 cloves garlic, minced

1 small shallot, minced

½ lb. sliced baby bella mushrooms

10-oz. bag fresh spinach

¼ cup shredded Gruyère cheese

Nonstick cooking spray

1 cup water

1. In a bowl, beat the eggs, salt, and pepper.

2. Gently fold in the basil, garlic, shallot, mushrooms, spinach, and cheese.

3. Spray a 7-inch round pan with nonstick cooking spray, then pour in the egg/vegetable/cheese mixture.

4. Pour the water into the bottom of the inner pot of the Instant Pot.

5. Place the 7-inch round pan on top of the trivet and slowly lower it into the Instant Pot using the handles.

6. Secure the lid and set the valve to sealing.

7. Set the Instant Pot to Manual and set the cooking time to 10 minutes.

8. When the cooking time is over, let the pressure release naturally, then remove the lid and remove the trivet and pan carefully with oven mitts.

9. Slice into 4 slices and serve warm.

Insta-Oatmeal

Hope Comerford, Clinton Township, MI

Makes 2 servings

Prep. Time: 2 minutes   *Cooking Time: 3 minutes*

1 cup gluten-free rolled oats

1 tsp. cinnamon

1 ½ Tbsp. maple syrup

Pinch salt

2 cups unsweetened almond milk

1. Place all ingredients in the inner pot of the Instant Pot and give a quick stir.

2. Secure the lid and set the vent to sealing.

3. Press the Manual button and set the cooking time to 3 minutes.

4. When the cooking time is up, manually release the pressure.

5. Remove the lid and stir. If the oatmeal is still too runny for you, let it sit a few minutes uncovered and it will thicken up.

Serving suggestion:

Top with ¼ cup of your favorite fruits, like banana slices, raspberries, chopped strawberries, or blueberries.

Berry Breakfast Parfait

Susan Tjon, Austin, TX

Makes 4 servings

Prep. Time: 15 minutes

2 cups vanilla yogurt

¼ tsp. ground cinnamon

1 cup sliced strawberries

½ cup blueberries

½ cup raspberries

1 cup low-sugar granola

1. Combine yogurt and cinnamon in small bowl.

2. Combine fruit in medium bowl.

3. For each parfait, layer ¼ cup fruit mixture, then 2 Tbsp. granola, followed by ¼ cup yogurt mixture in parfait glass (or whatever container you choose).

4. Repeat layers once more and top with a sprinkling of granola.

Soups, Stews & Chilies

Buffalo Chicken Veggie Chili

Maria Shevlin, Sicklerville, NJ

Makes 4 servings

Prep. Time: 10 minutes ⚬ Cooking Time: 20 minutes

1–2 lb. ground white meat chicken

1 Tbsp. olive oil

¼ cup thin-sliced carrots

¼ cup green beans, cut into small pieces

4 large mushrooms, chopped

½ cup onion, chopped fine

2–3 cloves garlic, minced

1 cup tomato sauce

¼ cup hot sauce

Salt and pepper to taste, if needed

1 Tbsp. fajita seasoning

1. Brown the meat, remove from pan, and cover to keep warm.

2. Heat olive oil in a pot, then add the carrots, green beans, mushrooms, onion, and garlic. Sauté until al dente.

3. Add the meat into the pot with all the remaining ingredients and mix well.

4. Simmer, covered, for approximately 5–10 minutes.

5. Serve and enjoy

Serving suggestion:

Feel free to top with fresh herbs or green onion and sour cream if desired.

Chicken Spinach Soup

Carna Reitz, Remington, VA

Makes 4–6 servings

Prep. Time: 5 minutes   *Cooking Time: 20 minutes*

6½ cups chicken broth, *divided*

2 cups cooked, chopped, or shredded chicken

1–2 cups frozen chopped spinach

Salt and pepper, to taste

½ cup flour

1. Put 6 cups broth, chicken, spinach, and salt and pepper in a large stockpot. Bring to a boil.

2. Meanwhile, mix flour and remaining ½ cup broth together in a jar. Put on lid and shake until smooth. When soup is boiling, slowly pour into soup to thicken, stirring constantly.

3. Continue stirring and cooking until soup thickens.

Ginger Chicken Noodle Soup

Hope Comerford, Clinton Township, MI

Makes 8 servings

Prep. Time: 5 minutes ⚬ *Cooking Time: 25 minutes*

2 Tbsp. olive oil

2 carrots, peeled and sliced into ¼-inch thick disks

2 stalks celery, diced

1 cup diced sweet onion

4 cloves garlic, minced

2 cups shredded rotisserie chicken meat

2 bay leaves

2 Tbsp. freshly chopped thyme

1½ Tbsp. freshly grated ginger

1 tsp. salt

¼ tsp. pepper

8 cups chicken stock

8-oz. package egg noodles

1. In a large stockpot, heat the olive oil.

2. Sauté the carrots, celery, onion, and garlic in the heated olive oil until the onion is translucent and the vegetables are softened (about 7–8 minutes).

3. Place the shredded chicken into the stockpot, along with the bay leaves, thyme, ginger, salt, pepper, and chicken stock.

4. Bring the contents to a boil and let boil for about 10 minutes.

5. Add in the egg noodles and continue to boil for approximately 10 additional minutes, or until the noodles have softened to your liking. Remove bay leaves before serving.

Tips:

You can prep the veggies ahead of time and store them in the refrigerator to save time. Taste and make any necessary seasoning adjustments. You may need more salt depending on how salty your broth and rotisserie chicken are.

Bean Soup with Turkey Sausage

STOVETOP

Dorothy Reise, Severna Park, MD
D. Fern Ruth, Chalfont, PA

Makes 4 servings

Prep. Time: 10 minutes ❧ Cooking Time: 15–20 minutes

8 oz. turkey kielbasa

4 cups chicken broth

2 (15-oz.) cans cannelloni beans, drained and rinsed

½–1 cup chopped onion

2 tsp. fresh minced basil

¼ tsp. coarsely ground pepper

1 clove garlic, minced

1 carrot, peeled and sliced, or 1 cup baby carrots

½ red, yellow, or orange bell pepper, sliced

3 cups fresh spinach, cleaned

¼ cup fresh chopped parsley

1. Cut turkey kielbasa lengthwise, and then into ½-inch slices. Sauté in Dutch oven or large saucepan until browned, stirring occasionally so it doesn't stick.

2. Combine all ingredients in pan except spinach and parsley.

3. Bring to boil, and then reduce heat. Cover and simmer 10–15 minutes, or until onion and carrots are tender.

4. If you're using frozen spinach, add it to the soup and let it thaw in the soup pot. Stir occasionally to break up spinach and to have it heat through. If you're using fresh spinach, remove stems from fresh spinach, stack, and cut into 1-inch strips. Remove soup from heat and stir in spinach and parsley until spinach wilts.

5. Serve immediately.

Variation:

For a thicker soup, remove 1 cup of hot soup after Step 3 and carefully process in firmly covered blender or food processor until smooth. Stir back into soup and continue with Step 4.

Broccoli Rabe and Sausage Soup

Carlene Horne, Bedford, NH

Makes 4 servings

Prep. Time: 10 minutes & *Cooking Time: 20 minutes*

2 Tbsp. olive oil

I onion, chopped

I lb. sweet or spicy sausage, casing removed, sliced

I bunch broccoli rabe, approximately 5 cups chopped

32 oz. chicken broth

I cup water

8 oz. frozen tortellini

1. In a stockpot, heat the olive oil.

2. Add the onion and sausage and sauté until tender.

3. Add the broccoli rabe and sauté for a few more minutes.

4. Pour the broth and water into the stockpot; bring to a simmer.

5. Add the tortellini and cook a few minutes until tender.

Tip:

Substitute any green, such as Swiss chard, kale, or spinach, for the broccoli rabe.

Serving suggestion:

Serve with grated cheese and crusty bread.

Sausage Chili

Norma I. Gehman, Ephrata, PA

Makes 4–6 servings

Prep. Time: 5 minutes ⚬ Cooking Time: 20–25 minutes

1 lb. loose sausage
¼ cup diced onion
2 Tbsp. flour
15½-oz. can chili beans in chili sauce
14½-oz. can diced tomatoes, undrained

1. Brown sausage in a large stockpot.

2. Add diced onion. Cook over medium heat until tender.

3. When onion is cooked, sprinkle 2 Tbsp. flour over mixture. Stir until flour is absorbed.

4. Add chili beans and diced tomatoes with juice. Mix well.

5. Simmer, covered, for 15 minutes.

Tips:

1. For more zip, use hot Italian sausage.
2. Crumble corn chips into the bottom of each serving bowl. Spoon chili over top of chips. Or crumble corn chips over top of each individual serving.
3. Grate your favorite cheese over top of each individual serving.
4. This recipe tastes even better when warmed up a day later.

Ham and Bean Soup

Diane Eby, Holtwood, PA

Makes 6–8 servings

Prep. Time: 5 minutes   Cooking Time: 15–20 minutes

1 qt. water
2 cups diced fully cooked ham
40½-oz. can great northern beans
½ lb. Velveeta cheese, cubed

1. Place water and ham in a large stockpot. Cook for 5 minutes.

2. Add beans. Heat through.

3. Add cheese. Stir until cheese melts.

Meatball Tortellini Soup

Lucille Amos, Greensboro, NC

Makes 4 servings

Prep. Time: 5 minutes ❧ *Cooking Time: 20–25 minutes*

14-oz. can beef broth
12 frozen Italian meatballs
1 cup stewed tomatoes
1-oz. can Mexican-style corn, drained
1 cup (20) frozen cheese tortellini

1. Bring broth to boil in a large stockpot.

2. Add meatballs. Cover and reduce heat. Simmer 5 minutes.

3. Add tomatoes and corn. Cover and simmer 5 minutes more.

4. Add tortellini. Cover and simmer 5 more minutes, or until tortellini is tender.

Note:

To make this recipe vegetarian, swap the beef broth for vegetable broth and swap the Italian meatballs for meatless meatballs.

Quick and Easy Chili

Carolyn Spohn, Shawnee, KS

Makes 3–4 servings

Prep. Time: 5 minutes ⚓ *Cooking Time: 25 minutes*

½ lb. ground beef or turkey, browned and drained

1 medium-sized onion, chopped

2 cloves garlic, minced

2 (15-oz.) cans chili-style beans, with liquid

8-oz. can tomato sauce

1. Brown ground beef in a large skillet.

2. Drain, leaving about 1 tsp. drippings in pan. Sauté onion and garlic until softened.

3. Add beans, with liquid, and the tomato sauce. Bring to a slow boil.

4. Reduce heat to simmer and cook for 15 minutes.

5. Return meat to skillet. Heat together for 5 minutes.

Beef and Black Bean Chili

STOVETOP

Eileen B. Jarvis, Saint Augustine, FL

Makes 8 servings

Prep. Time: 5 minutes · Cooking Time: 20 minutes

1 lb. lean ground beef

2 (15-oz.) cans black beans, rinsed and drained, *divided*

½ cup water

1 cup medium, or hot, chunky salsa

2 (8-oz.) cans no-salt-added tomato sauce

1 Tbsp. chili powder

Fresh cilantro, *optional*

Green onions, *optional*

Sour cream, *optional*

Cheddar cheese, grated, *optional*

1. Brown meat in large saucepan over medium-high heat. Drain off drippings.

2. While meat cooks, drain, rinse, and mash 1 can black beans.

3. Add mashed beans, second can of rinsed and drained beans, water, salsa, tomato sauce, and chili powder to saucepan. Stir well.

4. Cover. Cook over medium heat for 10 minutes. Stir occasionally.

5. If you wish, top individual servings with fresh cilantro, sliced green onions, sour cream, and/or cheese.

Black Bean and Mushroom Chili

Maria Shevlin, Sicklerville, NJ

Makes 4–6 servings

Prep. Time: 5 minutes ⚬ *Cooking Time: 25 minutes*

2 tsp. olive oil

4 cloves garlic, minced

1 large onion, diced

8-oz. pkg. mushrooms, chopped

15-oz. can black beans, drained and rinsed

2 (14½-oz.) cans petite diced tomatoes

1 can water

1 vegetable bouillon cube

1 tsp. cumin

1 Tbsp. garlic powder

1 Tbsp. onion powder

1 Tbsp. parsley flakes

2 tsp. paprika

1. In a large stock pot, add olive oil, garlic, and onion. Cook until softened (about 5 minutes) over medium heat. Stir often.

2. Add the mushrooms, stir, and cover. Cook for an additional 3–4 minutes.

3. Remove cover and add the remaining ingredients including all of the spices. Cover and simmer on low for an additional 15 minutes.

Serving suggestions:

Serve with any or all of the following:

- Steamed organic brown rice
- Green onion
- Plain Greek yogurt or sour cream
- Shredded sharp cheese

Creamy Broccoli Soup

SuAnne Burkholder, Millersburg, OH

Makes 3–4 servings

Prep. Time: 10 minutes ❧ Cooking Time: 15–20 minutes

4 cups milk, *divided*

1 Tbsp. chicken-flavored soup base

1½ cups cut-up broccoli

2 Tbsp. cornstarch

Salt to taste

1. Heat 3 cups milk and chicken base in a stockpot over low heat until hot.

2. Meanwhile, place cut-up broccoli in a microwave-safe dish. Add 1 Tbsp. water. Cover. Microwave on High for 1½ minutes. Stir. Repeat until broccoli becomes bright green and just-tender. Be careful not to overcook it! Drain broccoli of liquid.

3. In a small bowl, or in a jar with a tight-fitting lid, mix 1 cup milk and cornstarch until smooth. Slowly add to hot milk mixture.

4. Simmer gently, stirring constantly. When slightly thickened, add broccoli and salt.

Veggie Minestrone

Dorothy VanDeest, Memphis, TN

Makes 8 servings

Prep. Time: 15 minutes & *Cooking Time: 4 minutes*

2 Tbsp. olive oil

1 large onion, chopped

1 clove garlic, minced

4 cups low-sodium chicken or vegetable stock

16-oz. can kidney beans, rinsed and drained

14½-oz. can no-salt-added diced tomatoes

2 medium carrots, sliced thin

¼ tsp. dried oregano

¼ tsp. pepper

½ cup whole wheat elbow macaroni, uncooked

4 oz. fresh spinach

½ cup grated Parmesan cheese

1. Set the Instant Pot to the Sauté function and heat the olive oil.

2. When the olive oil is heated, add the onion and garlic to the inner pot and sauté for 5 minutes.

3. Press Cancel and add the stock, kidney beans, tomatoes, carrots, oregano, and pepper. Gently pour in the macaroni, but *do not stir.* Just push the noodles gently under the liquid.

4. Secure the lid and set the vent to sealing.

5. Manually set the cook time for 4 minutes on high pressure.

6. When the cooking time is over, manually release the pressure and remove the lid when the pin drops.

7. Stir in the spinach and let wilt a few minutes.

8. Sprinkle 1 Tbsp. grated Parmesan on each individual bowl of soup. Enjoy!

Flavorful Tomato Soup

Shari Ladd, Hudson, MI

Makes 4 servings

Prep. Time: 10 minutes   *Cooking Time: 20 minutes*

2 Tbsp. chopped onions

1 Tbsp. extra-virgin olive oil

3 Tbsp. flour

2 tsp. sugar

½ tsp. pepper

¼ tsp. dried basil

½ tsp. dried oregano

¼ tsp. dried thyme

1 qt. stewed tomatoes, no salt added, undrained

2 cups skim milk

1. Sauté onions in oil in stockpot.

2. Stir in flour and seasonings.

3. Stir in stewed tomatoes, stirring constantly. Bring to a boil and boil 1 minute.

4. Add 2 cups milk. If soup is too thick, add a little water. Stir well.

5. Simmer 10 minutes but do not boil.

Mamma Ree's Shrimp Chowda

Maria Shevlin, Sicklerville, NJ

Makes 4 servings

Prep. Time: 10 minutes   Cooking Time: 20 minutes

3 tsp. avocado or olive oil, *divided*

10–20 medium-to-large shrimp, peeled and deveined

1 cup mushrooms, sliced and cut in half

1½ cups thin-sliced yellow bell peppers

8-oz. bag fresh spinach

1 cup sliced onions

3 cloves garlic, minced

Salt to taste

Pepper to taste

1 tsp. garlic powder

1 tsp. onion powder

1 Tbsp. parsley

1 tsp. salt

½ tsp. black pepper

¼–1 tsp. red pepper flakes, according to your spice level

1 cup heavy cream

2–4 oz. seafood or vegetable stock

1. In a pan, heat 2 tsp. of oil. Sauté the shrimp lightly for 1 minute on both sides. Remove and keep warm.

2. Add the remaining teaspoon of oil to the pan, along with the mushrooms, bell peppers, spinach, onion, garlic, and all of the spices. Sauté until your desired tenderness.

3. Add the cream and seafood or vegetable stock. Stir well.

4. Place the shrimp back into the pan along with any juices that may have accumulated. Simmer for approximately 5 minutes over low heat.

Note:

Tastes like a fancy seafood chowder!

Oyster Stew

Dorothy Reise, Severna Park, MD

Makes 4 servings

Prep. Time: 10–15 minutes   Cooking Time: 15 minutes

2–3 dozen fresh oysters in liquid
2 Tbsp. butter
1 Tbsp. chopped onion
3 Tbsp. flour
3 cups milk
1 tsp. salt
½ tsp. pepper
½ tsp. chopped parsley
Pinch celery seed, *optional*
Dash paprika, *optional*

1. In a small skillet over medium heat, precook oysters in their own liquid until edges curl and oysters become plump. Set aside.

2. In large stockpot, melt butter, add onion, and sauté until soft.

3. Over medium heat, add flour and stir until smooth.

4. Slowly add milk, stirring constantly until thickened.

5. Add the cooked oysters and liquid, salt, pepper, and parsley, and celery seed and paprika if you wish. Mix well.

6. Heat thoroughly and serve.

Salads

Tossed Taco Salad

Maxine "Meme" Phaneuf, Washington, MI

Makes 10 large servings

Prep. Time: 10 minutes ⚬ *Cooking Time: 15 minutes*

1 Tbsp. olive oil

1 small onion, chopped

2½ lb. ground turkey

1 Tbsp. oregano

1 tsp. cumin

6½-oz. can sliced black olives, drained

13 oz. can dark red kidney beans

2 (15½-oz.) cans pinto beans, drained

2 heads iceberg lettuce, torn or chopped

2 cups shredded cheese

8 oz. tortilla chips, crushed

Jalapeño slices, *optional*

Dressing:

2 cups nonfat mayonnaise

½ cup taco sauce

1 tsp. hot sauce

1. In a large skillet, heat the olive oil.

2. When the oil is hot, sauté the onion for 2 minutes, then add in the ground turkey. Season with the oregano and cumin. Sauté for about 15 minutes, or until cooked through.

3. In a large bowl, add the remaining ingredients, then stir in the browned turkey meat.

4. Assemble the dressing in a small bowl, then pour over the turkey mixture in the large bowl and toss to coat evenly.

5. Serve and enjoy!

Tip:

Because this recipe makes so many servings, it's great for a crowd, or even for prepping lunches for the week.

Grilled Fiesta Chicken Salad

STOVETOP **GRILL**

Liz Clapper, Lancaster, PA

Makes 4 main-dish servings

Prep. Time: 10 minutes · Cooking Time: 20 minutes

1 head Bibb lettuce

1 head red leaf lettuce

1 cup shredded carrots

1 medium tomato, diced

2 green onions, chopped

1 lb. boneless, skinless chicken breasts

1 tsp. chili powder

1 sweet red bell pepper

1 Tbsp. olive oil

1 cup thawed frozen corn

½ cup shredded low-fat cheddar cheese

8 Tbsp. fat-free ranch dressing

2 whole wheat pita breads, 4-inch diameter

1. Tear up heads of lettuce and toss together in a large bowl. Top with shredded carrots, diced tomato, and chopped green onions.

2. Season chicken with chili powder. Grill chicken 3–4 minutes on each side.

3. Meanwhile, dice red pepper. Toss with olive oil and cook in a medium skillet over medium heat for 2 minutes.

4. Add corn and cook for 1 more minute.

5. When chicken has cooled to room temperature, dice chicken.

6. Top salad with diced chicken.

7. Spoon corn and pepper over top.

8. Sprinkle with cheese. Drizzle each salad with 2 Tbsp. dressing.

9. Grill whole wheat pitas for 2–3 minutes each side. Cut into fourths. Serve 2 wedges with each individual salad.

Tip:

You can bake pitas at 375°F in oven for 10 minutes instead of grilling.

Greek Salad

Ruth Feister, Narvon, PA

Makes 4 servings

Prep. Time: 20 minutes

Dressing:

¼ cup chicken stock

2 Tbsp. red wine vinegar

2 tsp. lemon juice

1 tsp. sugar

1 tsp. fresh minced basil

¾ tsp. fresh minced oregano

Salad:

Head of torn romaine lettuce

12 oz. cooked rotisserie chicken, chopped

1 medium-sized cucumber, sliced thin

2 medium-sized tomatoes, cut in pieces

½ red onion, finely chopped

¼ cup chopped fresh parsley

4-oz. can sliced black olives, drained

3–4 oz. crumbled feta cheese

Several artichoke hearts, quartered

1. Combine dressing ingredients in a jar with a tightly fitting lid. Shake until mixed well.

2. Place lettuce, chicken, cucumber, tomatoes, onions, and parsley in a large serving bowl.

3. Just before serving, drizzle with dressing and toss.

4. Top with olives, cheese, and artichoke hearts.

Almond-Apricot Chicken Salad

(STOVETOP)

Tracey Hanson Schramel, Windom, MN

Makes 6–8 servings

Prep. Time: 15 minutes   Cooking Time: 15 minutes

Salad:

½ lb. bowtie pasta

3 cups chopped broccoli

2½ cups chopped, cooked chicken

1 cup chopped celery

1 cup dried apricots, cut into ¼-inch strips

¾ cup toasted whole almonds

½ cup finely chopped green onions

Dressing:

¾ cup mayonnaise

¾ cup sour cream

2 tsp. grated lemon peel

1 Tbsp. lemon juice

1 Tbsp. Dijon-style mustard

1 tsp. salt

¼ tsp. pepper

1. Cook pasta according to directions on the box. Once done, drain and rinse.

2. Meanwhile, in a large bowl, combine salad ingredients.

2. In another bowl, combine dressing ingredients.

3. When the pasta is drained and rinsed, add to the bowl and then pour dressing over pasta mixture and toss.

Tips:

1. Instead of stirring the almonds into the salad, sprinkle them on top if you like that look better.

2. Pass the dressing in a small pitcher so each person can put on the amount they like. The leftovers don't get soggy then, either!

Caesar Salad

Colleen Heatwole, Burton, MI

Makes 4 servings

Prep Time: 15–20 minutes

8–12 cups romaine lettuce, or spring mix, torn into bite-sized pieces

12 oz. cooked rotisserie chicken, chopped

⅓ cup oil

3 Tbsp. red wine vinegar

1 tsp. Worcestershire sauce

½ tsp. salt

¾ tsp. dry mustard powder

1 large clove garlic, minced

1½–2 Tbsp. fresh lemon juice

Dash pepper

¼–½ cup grated Parmesan cheese

2 cups Caesar-flavored, or garlic, croutons

1. Place lettuce and chicken in a large bowl.

2. Combine next 6 ingredients in a blender or food processor.

3. Add fresh lemon juice and process until smooth.

4. Just before serving, toss with lettuce.

5. Sprinkle with pepper. Add Parmesan cheese and toss well. Serve croutons separately.

Asparagus, Apple, and Chicken Salad

Betty Salch, Bloomington, IL
Wilma Stoltzfus, Honey Brook, PA

Makes 3–4 servings

Prep Time: 20 minutes   Cooking Time: 3–4 minutes

1 cup fresh asparagus, cut into 1-inch-long pieces

2 Tbsp. cider vinegar

2 Tbsp. vegetable oil

2 tsp. honey

2 tsp. minced fresh parsley

½ tsp. salt

¼ tsp. pepper

1 cup cubed cooked chicken

½ cup diced red apples, unpeeled

2 cups torn mixed greens alfalfa sprouts, *optional*

1. In a small saucepan, cook asparagus in a small amount of water until crisp-tender, about 3–4 minutes. Drain and cool.

2. In a good-sized mixing bowl, combine the next 6 ingredients.

3. Stir in the chicken, apples, and asparagus. Toss.

4. Serve over greens. Garnish with alfalfa sprouts if you wish.

Chicken Salad with Blue Cheese

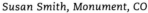

NO-COOK

Susan Smith, Monument, CO

Makes 4–6 servings

Prep. Time: 15 minutes

3 cups diced rotisserie chicken meat

6 cups shredded lettuce

1–2 cups mayonnaise

2 Tbsp. tarragon vinegar

4 Tbsp. chili sauce, or cocktail sauce

2 Tbsp. chopped green bell pepper

4 oz. blue cheese, crumbled

Whole lettuce leaves

1. Mix chicken with shredded lettuce.

2. Mix mayonnaise, vinegar, chili sauce, and bell pepper. Add crumbled blue cheese.

3. Gently combine chicken and mayonnaise mixtures.

4. Place salad in a bowl lined with lettuce or in individual lettuce cups.

Tips:

1. White meat chicken is ideal for this salad.

2. The salad is best made and eaten on the same day.

Curried Chicken Salad

Bonita Stutzman, Harrisonburg, VA

Makes 10 main-dish servings

Prep. Time: 20 minutes

I cup mayonnaise

¾ cup plain yogurt

2 Tbsp. honey

I Tbsp. lemon juice

1½ Tbsp. curry powder

6 cups chopped rotisserie chicken meat, cooled

3 cups halved red grapes

¾ cup toasted slivered almonds

¾ cup diced celery

Romaine lettuce

1. Mix together the first five ingredients in a medium bowl.

2. In a large bowl, toss together chicken, grapes, almonds, and celery.

3. Pour dressing over chicken mixture and toss.

4. Refrigerate until serving time.

5. Serve on a bed of romaine lettuce.

Orange-Spinach Chicken Salad

Esther Shisler, Lansdale, PA

Makes 4–6 servings

Prep. Time: 25 minutes

Honey-Caraway Dressing:

¾ cup mayonnaise

2 Tbsp. honey

1 Tbsp. lemon juice

1 Tbsp. caraway seeds

Salad:

10-oz. bag spinach or romaine

1 medium head iceberg lettuce, shredded

3 cups shredded cooked rotisserie chicken

2 Tbsp. diced onion

2 Tbsp. diced jarred pimento, or red bell pepper

2 large oranges, peeled and chopped

1 small cucumber, sliced

1. In small bowl, whisk mayonnaise, honey, lemon juice, and caraway seeds until blended. Cover and refrigerate. Stir before using.

2. Into large salad bowl, tear spinach or romaine into bite-sized pieces.

3. Add shredded chicken, lettuce, onion, pimento, oranges, and cucumber. Toss gently with dressing.

Tip:
A 15-oz. can mandarin oranges, drained, can be used instead of the 2 oranges.

Serving suggestion:
Goes well with lasagna and pasta dishes as a side if you wish.

Salad with Hot Bacon Dressing

Joanne E. Martin, Stevens, PA

Makes 8–10 servings (2 cups dressing)

Prep. Time: 15 minutes ⚬ Cooking Time: 15 minutes

6–8 strips of bacon

1½ cups sugar

2 eggs, beaten

⅓ cup vinegar

⅔ cup water

Salad greens

Grated carrots

Hard-cooked eggs

1. In a skillet, brown bacon. Drain off drippings. Crumble and set aside.

2. In the same skillet, mix sugar, beaten eggs, vinegar, and water. Bring to boil, stirring up browned bacon drippings. Stir dressing until slightly thickened.

3. Stir in bacon.

4. Just before serving, toss warm salad dressing with mixture of salad greens, grated carrots, and hard-cooked eggs.

BLT Pasta Salad

Bernadette Veenstra, Grand Rapids, MI

Makes 12–16 servings

Prep. Time: 5 minutes ⚘ *Cooking Time: 25 minutes*

6 cups water

16-oz. pkg. rigatoni, or penne, pasta

1 lb. bacon, diced

1 pt. cherry tomatoes, quartered

7-oz. bag fresh spinach, roughly chopped

1 tsp. salt

¼ tsp. black pepper

8 oz. shredded mozzarella cheese, *optional*

1. Set water to boil for the pasta. While this is happening, move on to the next steps in order to keep this recipe under 30 minutes. Keep an eye on the water and, once boiling, add the pasta to cook for the recommended time on the package.

2. Meanwhile, sauté bacon pieces over medium heat. Once cooked, place bacon on paper towel–lined plate. Pour all drippings into a small bowl.

3. Return 1½ Tbsp. drippings to skillet and heat. Add the tomatoes to skillet and sauté for a few minutes. Add spinach into hot drippings until it wilts, about 1 minute.

4. Drain your pasta and run under cool water. Pour into a large bowl.

5. Transfer tomato and spinach to pasta. Add salt, pepper, and mozzarella cheese if desired. Stir.

6. If pasta seems dry, add up to 1½ Tbsp. more of the drippings.

Pasta Salad with Tuna

Sheila Soldner, Lititz, PA

Makes 6–8 servings

Prep. Time: 15 minutes ☙ *Cooking Time: 15 minutes*

½ lb. uncooked rotini pasta

12½-oz. can solid white tuna, drained and flaked

2 cups thinly sliced cucumber

1 large tomato, seeded and sliced, or ½ pt. cherry or grape tomatoes

½ cup sliced celery

¼ cup chopped green bell pepper

¼ cup sliced green onions

1 cup bottled Italian dressing

¼ cup mayonnaise

1 Tbsp. prepared mustard

1 tsp. dill weed

1 tsp. salt

⅛ tsp. pepper

1. Prepare rotini according to package directions. Drain.

2. In a large bowl, combine rotini, tuna, cucumbers, tomato, celery, green pepper, and onions.

3. In a small bowl, blend the Italian dressing, mayonnaise, mustard, and seasonings. Add to salad mixture. Toss to coat.

4. Cover and chill. Toss gently before serving.

Albacore Tuna-Stuffed Tomatoes

NO-COOK

Joe Barker, Carlsbad, NM

Makes 6–8 servings

Prep. Time: 15–20 minutes

6–8 Roma tomatoes

2 (6-oz.) cans albacore tuna, drained

1 Tbsp. mayonnaise

½ tsp. prepared mustard

1½ tsp. blue cheese dressing

2 tsp. thinly sliced green onion

1½ tsp. chopped chives

1½ tsp. chopped black olives

1½ tsp. chopped cucumber

1½ tsp. chopped red bell pepper

1½ tsp. chopped yellow bell pepper

celery leaves

Sprinkle of paprika

6–8 mint leaves

1. Cut tomatoes in half and remove seeds and veins. Keep for another use. Keep the tomato shells cool.

2. Mix remaining ingredients except paprika and mint together in a bowl.

3. Stuff tomato halves with tuna mixture.

4. Sprinkle paprika lightly over top.

5. Garnish each tomato with a mint leaf.

Main Dishes

Chicken

Chicken with Bacon & Onion Sauce

Maria Shevlin, Sicklerville, NJ

Makes 4 servings

Prep. Time: 5 minutes ✧ Cooking Time: 25 minutes

1 tsp. olive oil

1 small onion, chopped

4–5 cloves garlic, grated or minced

4 slices bacon, chopped

1 Tbsp. butter

4 boneless skinless chicken thighs, chopped into bite-size pieces

⅓ tsp. salt

⅛ tsp. pepper

⅓ cup chicken stock or bone broth

1½ Tbsp. cream cheese

Sprinkle parsley flakes

1. Add oil, onion, garlic, and bacon to a large nonstick fry pan. Cook over low heat, stirring frequently until bacon is crisp but not burnt, approximately 10 minutes. Remove from pan and place in a bowl. Cover to keep warm.

2. Add the butter and chicken to the pan. Cover and cook about 10 minutes, turning the pieces occasionally to cook on all sides.

3. Add the chicken stock, cream cheese, and the bacon/onion mixture. Once the cream cheese is melted, plate the chicken.

4. Sprinkle each serving with a bit of parsley.

Serving suggestion:

Serve with roasted broccoli, green beans, or mashed cauliflower/potatoes.

Crispy Ranch Chicken

OVEN

Barb Shirk, Hawkins, WI
Arlene Snyder, Millerstown, PA
Doyle Rounds, Bridgewater, VA
Pat Chase, Fairbank, IA

Makes 6–8 servings

Prep. Time: 5 minutes ⚬ *Baking Time: 20–25 minutes*

¾–2 cups crispy rice cereal

¾ cup grated Parmesan cheese

1-oz. envelope dry ranch dressing mix

2 egg whites, beaten

8 (5-oz.) boneless, skinless chicken thighs, halved into thinner pieces

1. Preheat oven to 350°F.

2. Spray a large baking sheet with nonstick cooking spray.

3. Combine rice cereal, Parmesan cheese, and dry dressing mix in a large bowl.

4. Place beaten egg whites in a medium-sized bowl.

5. Dip each chicken thigh in the egg whites, and then in the cereal.

6. Arrange the coated chicken on the prepared baking sheet.

7. Bake for about 20–25 minutes, or until chicken is golden and juices run clear when meat is pierced with a knife.

Garlic Chicken Cutlets

Elaine Vigoda, Rochester, NY

Makes 6 servings

Prep. Time: 10 minutes ⚬ Cooking Time: 20 minutes

4 chicken cutlets, approx. 1 ½ lb.

2 Tbsp. flour or matzo meal

1 Tbsp. oil

6–8 cloves garlic, peeled and very lightly crushed

½ lb. fresh mushrooms, any combination of varieties, cut into pieces or slices

¼ cup balsamic vinegar

¾ cup chicken stock

1 bay leaf

3 sprigs fresh thyme, chopped

1 tsp. apricot jam

1. Dust chicken lightly with matzo meal or flour.

2. In large skillet, heat the oil over medium-high heat and add garlic. Sauté about 3 minutes, until browned.

3. Remove with a slotted spoon and reserve.

4. Add chicken to skillet and brown on one side for 3 minutes.

5. Turn chicken and top with reserved garlic and mushrooms. Cook 3 minutes.

6. While chicken is cooking, mix the vinegar, chicken stock, bay leaf, thyme, and jam in a small bowl. Pour over chicken and vegetables.

7. Reduce heat to low, cover the skillet, and cook approximately 10 minutes, or until chicken is done. Remove bay leaf before serving.

Chicken Breasts with Fresh Fruit

Robin Schrock, Millersburg, OH

Makes 4 servings

Prep. Time: 15 minutes   Cooking Time: 15 minutes

1½ Tbsp. olive oil

½ tsp. salt

½ tsp. pepper

1 clove garlic, minced

4 large boneless, skinless chicken breast halves

¼ cup butter

1 cup fresh pineapple chunks

1 cup fresh, quartered strawberries

1 kiwi, peeled, quartered, and sliced

¼ cup chopped red onions

½ (4-oz.) can chopped green chilies

1 tsp. cornstarch

⅓ cup freshly squeezed orange juice

1. In a small bowl, combine oil, salt, pepper, and garlic. Spread over one side of each chicken breast.

2. In skillet, sauté chicken in butter, seasoned side down, 4–6 minutes. Turn and cook another 4–6 minutes, or until chicken juices run clear.

3. While chicken is sautéing, cut up fruit and onions into mixing bowl. Stir in chilies.

4. In a small bowl, combine cornstarch and juice until smooth.

5. Remove cooked chicken from skillet to serving platter. Keep warm. Stir juice mixture into skillet and bring to a boil. Cook and stir for 1–2 minutes, or until thickened. Remove from heat and pour over fruit/onion/chilies mixture. Gently toss to coat.

6. Serve about ⅓ cup fruit sauce over each chicken breast.

Honey Mustard Chicken

Rhoda Nissley, Parkesburg, PA

Makes 4 servings

Prep. Time: 5 minutes ⚭ Cooking Time: 20 minutes

½ cup Miracle Whip salad dressing

2 Tbsp. prepared mustard

1 Tbsp. honey

4 boneless, skinless chicken breast halves

1. In a small mixing bowl, stir salad dressing, mustard, and honey together.

2. Place chicken on grill or rack of broiler pan. Brush with half the sauce.

3. Grill or broil 8–10 minutes. Turn and brush with remaining sauce.

4. Continue grilling or broiling 8–10 minutes, or until tender.

Lemon Grilled Chicken Breasts

GRILL

Wilma Haberkamp, Fairbank, IA

Makes 4 servings

Prep. Time: 15 minutes ⚬ *Cooking Time: 4–5 minutes*

1 ¼ lb. boneless, skinless chicken breasts

2 lemons

2 Tbsp. olive oil

½ tsp. salt

½ tsp. coarsely ground pepper

1. Prepare grill for direct grilling over medium heat.

2. Pound chicken to uniform ¼-inch thickness.

3. Grate 1½ Tbsp. lemon peel and squeeze 3 Tbsp. lemon juice into a small bowl.

4. Add oil, salt, and pepper. Whisk until well blended.

5. In large bowl, toss chicken with marinade.

6. Place chicken on grill. Cook 2–2½ minutes.

7. Turn over. Cook 2–2½ minutes more, or until juices run clear.

Chicken Scaloppine

STOVETOP

Betsy Chutchian, Grand Prairie, TX

Makes 6–8 servings

Prep. Time: 5-10 minutes ⚬ Cooking Time: 20 minutes

6–8 boneless, skinless chicken breast halves

½ tsp. salt

¼ tsp. pepper

¼ cup flour

7 Tbsp. butter, *divided*

¼ lb. fresh mushrooms, sliced, *divided*

2 tsp. fresh lemon juice

2 Tbsp. olive oil, *divided*

¼ lb. ham, cut into thin strips

½ cup dry sherry

½ cup chicken broth

Tip:
You can make this in one pan, but it will most likely take longer than 30 minutes.

1. Place chicken breasts between 2 sheets of plastic wrap and pound with a mallet or rolling pin to flatten.

2. Place salt, pepper, and flour in shallow bowl. Dip each breast half into mixture, coating both sides well.

3. Melt 3 tablespoons butter between 2 skillets. Add half of the mushrooms to each skillet and sauté about 5 minutes.

4. Remove mushrooms and sprinkle with lemon juice. Set aside.

5. Heat remaining butter and oil in skillets. Add several chicken breasts to each skillet (do not crowd them), and sauté until lightly browned on both sides. Remove chicken pieces as they brown and keep them warm on a platter covered with foil.

6. In one skillet, warm/brown the ham for a couple minutes, then set aside with the chicken to keep warm.

7. In the other skillet, add the sherry and broth and bring to a boil for 5 minutes, scraping up any bits from the bottom of the pan.

8. Serve the chicken, ham, and mushrooms on a large serving platter with the sauce over the top.

Jerk-Seasoned Chicken and Pepper Sauté

Louise Bodziony, Sunrise Beach, MO

Makes 4 servings

Prep. Time: 5–10 minutes ⚬ *Cooking Time: 15–20 minutes*

1 lb. boneless, skinless chicken breast halves, cut into ¾-inch-wide strips

2 tsp. Caribbean jerk seasoning

1 pkg. frozen bell pepper and onion stir fry

⅓ cup orange juice

2 tsp. cornstarch

1. Spray large nonstick skillet lightly with cooking spray. Heat over medium heat until hot.

2. Add chicken and jerk seasoning. Cook and stir 5–7 minutes, or until chicken is no longer pink.

3. Add pepper and onion stir fry. Cover and cook 3–5 minutes, or until vegetables are crisp-tender. Stir occasionally.

4. Meanwhile, in a small bowl, combine orange juice and cornstarch. Blend until smooth. Add to mixture in skillet; cook and stir until bubbly and thickened.

Serving suggestion:
This is good served over cooked rice.

Honey Orange Garlic Chicken

Maria Shevlin, Sicklerville, NJ

Makes 2–3 servings

Prep. Time: 5–10 minutes ❀ Cooking Time: 20–25 minutes

1–2 Tbsp. olive oil, *divided*
1 small onion, cubed
3 cloves garlic, diced fine
1 yellow bell pepper, cubed
1 section of fresh broccoli, separated
6 oz. chicken breast, diced
½ tsp. paprika
1 tsp. salt
½ tsp. black pepper
1 tsp. garlic powder
1 Tbsp. parsley flakes
¼ cup honey
1–2 True Orange crystallized orange packets
½ tsp. cornstarch
1 Tbsp. cold water

1. Lightly coat a wok or large frying pan with olive oil. Add the onion, garlic, pepper, and broccoli, and stir-fry for approximately 3–4 minutes over medium low heat. Remove the veggies to a bowl, lightly cover to keep warm, and set aside.

2. Add a little more oil to the wok or frying pan, then add the chicken with the paprika, salt, pepper, garlic powder, and parsley flakes. Cook until about 90 percent done, and then reintroduce the veggies in the covered bowl to the pan, with any liquid that may have developed in the bowl. Finish cooking.

3. Add in the honey. Start with ¼ cup and mix well. Cook for 3 minutes over low heat.

4. Add 1–2 True Orange crystallized orange packets and mix well. (This is to taste as well—you want just a slight orange flavor, and not for it to be overwhelming.)

5. Mix the cornstarch and water, then add this to the pan. Let it thicken for a couple minutes.

Serving suggestion:

Serve over instant rice if you choose.

Honey-Chicken Stir Fry

Anya Kauffman, Sheldon, WI

Makes 6 servings

Prep. Time: 15 minutes   Cooking Time: 10 minutes

1 lb. boneless skinless chicken breast

2 Tbsp. canola oil, *divided*

4 cups sliced raw vegetables (your choice of a combination of cabbage, onion, celery, carrots, broccoli, cauliflower, and sweet peppers)

Sauce:

1½ cups orange juice

⅔ cup honey

1 Tbsp. low-sodium soy sauce

2 Tbsp. cornstarch

½ tsp. ground ginger

1. Slice chicken breast into thin strips. Set aside.

2. Combine sauce ingredients in a bowl.

3. In a large skillet, stir-fry meat in 1 Tbsp. oil until no longer pink. Remove from skillet and set aside.

4. In remaining oil and in same skillet, stir-fry vegetables on high heat until crisp-tender.

5. Stir in meat and sauce until sauce is somewhat thickened.

Serving suggestion:

Serve over hot brown rice if you choose.

Encore Dijon Chicken

Dorothy VanDeest, Memphis, TN

Makes 4–6 servings

Prep. Time: 5 minutes ☙ Baking Time: 20 minutes

½ tsp. Italian seasoning

4 Tbsp. Dijon mustard

2 Tbsp. vegetable oil

1 tsp. garlic powder, or refrigerated minced garlic

4–6 boneless chicken breast halves, about 6-oz. each in weight

1. Grease a 7 × 11-inch or 9 × 13-inch baking dish.

2. Mix Italian seasoning, mustard, oil, and garlic in either a large bowl or plastic bag.

3. Add chicken pieces, one at a time. Dredge or shake to coat each piece.

4. Lay in baking dish.

5. Bake at 375°F for 20 minutes, or until thermometer inserted in center of each piece registers 165°F.

Curried Chicken Casserole

Marilyn Mowry, Irving, TX
Penelope Blosser, Beavercreek, OH

Makes 4–6 servings

Prep. Time: 5 minutes ♣ *Cooking Time: 20 minutes*

I cup long-grain rice, uncooked

I Tbsp. butter

I low-sodium chicken bouillon cube

2½ cups water

2 (5-oz.) cans chunk white chicken, drained, or 1½ cups cooked chicken breast

⅓ cup raisins

I tsp. curry powder

1. In a saucepan, sauté rice in butter,

2. Stir in bouillon cube and water.

3. Cover. Bring to boil.

4. Reduce heat and simmer, covered, 15 minutes, or until water is absorbed and rice is soft.

5. Stir in chicken, raisins, and curry powder, mixing well.

6. Cover saucepan. Remove from heat and let stand 10 minutes.

7. Fluff mixture with fork. Serve.

Easy Chicken Fajitas

Jessica Hontz, Coatesville, PA

Makes 4–6 servings

Prep. Time: 10 minutes   Cooking Time: 15–20 minutes

1 lb. boneless, skinless chicken breasts
1 pkg. dry Italian salad dressing mix
¼ cup Italian salad dressing
1 cup salsa
1 green bell pepper, sliced
½ medium-sized onion, sliced
10 (10-inch) flour tortillas

Optional Toppings:
Shredded Monterey Jack cheese
Shredded lettuce
Sour cream
Chopped tomatoes
Salsa
Hot pepper sauce
Jalapeño slices

1. Cut chicken into thin strips. Place in large mixing bowl.

2. Add dry salad dressing mix and salad dressing. Mix well.

3. In a large skillet, combine chicken strips, salsa, and pepper and onion slices. Stir-fry until chicken is cooked and peppers and onions are soft.

4. Place chicken mix in tortillas with your choice of toppings.

Easy Enchilada Chicken

Hope Comerford, Clinton Township, MI

Makes 10–14 servings

Prep. Time: 5 minutes ⚬ *Cooking Time: 10 minutes*

2 lb. boneless skinless chicken breasts, diced

½ cup chicken stock

14½-oz. can petite diced tomatoes

1 medium onion, chopped

8 ounces red enchilada sauce

½ teaspoon salt

½ teaspoon chili powder

½ teaspoon basil

½ teaspoon garlic powder

¼ teaspoon pepper

1. Place all ingredients into the inner pot of the Instant Pot.

2. Seal the lid and set the vent to sealing.

3. Manually set the cook time for 10 minutes on high pressure.

4. When cook time is up, let the pressure release naturally for 5 minutes, then manually release the remaining pressure.

Serving suggestion:

Serve over salad, brown rice, quinoa, or sweet potatoes.

Enchiladas the Easy Way

Hope Comerford, Clinton Township, MI

Makes 4 servings

Prep. Time: 10 minutes ⚬ *Cooking Time: 15 minutes*

2 cups shredded cooked chicken

4-oz. can diced green chilies

½ cup salsa

8 (8-inch) flour tortillas

10-oz. can red enchilada sauce

1 cup shredded Mexican blend cheese

1. Preheat the oven to 375°F.

2. Meanwhile, mix the shredded chicken with the diced green chilies and salsa.

3. Evenly fill each tortilla with the chicken mixture. Roll them up.

4. Spray a 13 × 9-inch baking dish with nonstick spray, then place the filled and rolled tortillas, seam side down, in the dish.

5. Pour the enchilada sauce over the top, then spread the cheese over that.

6. Bake for 15 minutes.

Honey-Baked Chicken Strips

Jan Rankin, Millersville, PA

Makes 3–4 servings

Prep. Time: 15 minutes ❦ *Baking Time: 15 minutes*

2 egg whites
1 Tbsp. honey
2 cups cornflake crumbs
¼–½ tsp. salt or garlic powder
1 lb. chicken tenders, cut into strips

1. Mix egg whites and honey together in a shallow bowl.

2. Place cornflake crumbs and seasoning in another shallow bowl.

3. Dip chicken strips into egg white–honey mixture.

4. Coat each strip with cornflake crumbs.

5. Place each strip on ungreased cookie sheet and bake at 400°F for 15 minutes.

Basil Chicken Strips

Melissa Raber, Millersburg, OH

Makes 2 servings

Prep. Time: 10 minutes ⚬ Cooking Time: 10 minutes

½ lb. boneless, skinless chicken breasts, cut into ¾-inch-wide strips

2 Tbsp. flour

3 Tbsp. butter

2 Tbsp. red wine vinegar or cider vinegar

½ tsp. dried basil

1. In a large resealable plastic bag, shake chicken strips and flour until coated.

2. In a large skillet over medium high heat, melt butter. Add chicken. Sauté for 5 minutes.

3. Stir in the vinegar and basil. Cook until chicken juices run clear.

Chicken Scampi à la Mamma

Maria Shevlin, Sicklerville, NJ

Makes 4 servings

Prep. Time: 5–8 minutes   *Cooking Time: 20–22 minutes*

6 cups water

8 oz. uncooked spaghetti

2 Tbsp. butter

1 Tbsp. olive oil

3 Tbsp. garlic, chopped fine

2 red bell peppers, cut into thin strips

1 vegetable bouillon cube dissolved in 1 cup hot water

¼ cup white wine or chicken stock

2 tsp. Italian seasoning

½ tsp. black pepper

1 tsp. garlic powder

1 medium onion, cut into thin strips

2–3 chicken breasts, cut thin, and into small pieces

1. Start water to boil in a pan. While waiting for it to come to a boil, continue on with the remaining directions. When the water does boil, cook the pasta according to the directions on the box.

2. Add butter, oil, and chopped garlic to large pan. Cook approximately 3 minutes.

3. Add the remaining ingredients. Simmer, covered, approximately 20–22 minutes, turning the chicken occasionally.

4. Serve over the freshly cooked pasta.

Serving suggestion:

Serve over rice instead of pasta if you choose.

Chicken and Bows

Arianne Hochstetler, Goshen, IN

Makes 12 servings

Prep. Time: 10 minutes   *Cooking Time: 20 minutes*

16-oz. pkg. bowtie pasta

2 lb. uncooked boneless, skinless chicken breasts, cut into strips

1 cup chopped red bell pepper

4 Tbsp. butter

2 (10¾-oz.) cans cream of chicken soup

2 cups frozen peas

1½ cups milk

1 tsp. garlic powder

¼–½ tsp. salt

¼ tsp. pepper

⅔ cup grated Parmesan cheese

1. Cook pasta according to package directions. Drain.

2. In large saucepan, cook chicken and red pepper in butter for 5–6 minutes until juices run clear.

3. Stir in soup, peas, milk, garlic powder, salt, and pepper.

4. Bring to boil. Simmer, uncovered, 1–2 minutes.

5. Stir in Parmesan cheese.

6. Add pasta and toss to coat.

7. Serve immediately, or refrigerate or freeze.

Tip:

This freezes well. To reheat from frozen: Thaw casserole in refrigerator overnight. Place in microwave-safe dish. Cover, and microwave 8–10 minutes or until heated through, stirring once. Or warm thawed dish in oven—350°F for 1 hour, or until bubbly and heated through.

Chicken Alfredo

STOVETOP

Erma Martin, East Earl, PA

Makes 4 servings

Prep. Time: 10 minutes   *Cooking Time: 15–20 minutes*

6 cups water

8 oz. uncooked fettuccine

8-oz. pkg. cream cheese, cubed

¾ cup milk, *divided*

½ tsp. garlic powder

Salt to taste

Pepper to taste

4 skinless, boneless, chicken breast
halves, cooked and diced

1. Start water to boil in a pan. While waiting for it to come to a boil, continue on with the remaining directions. When the water does boil, cook the pasta according to the directions on the box.

2. In a skillet over medium heat, melt the cream cheese in about ⅓ cup of the milk, stirring until smooth.

3. Add the remaining milk, the garlic powder, the salt, and the pepper. Cook for about 3 minutes until thickened.

4. Add the diced chicken and cook until the chicken is well heated, about 3 minutes.

5. Serve over the freshly cooked pasta.

Variation:

Add 2–3 cups thawed chopped broccoli to Step 3. Extend cooking time for that step to 5–7 minutes.

Tip:

Begin heating the cooking water for the fettuccine when you begin Step 1.

Chicken Alfredo Penne

Esther Gingerich, Parnell, IA

Makes 4 servings

Prep. Time: 5–8 minutes ⚬ Cooking Time: 15 minutes

½ lb. uncooked penne pasta

1 ½ cups frozen sugar snap peas

15-oz. jar Alfredo sauce

2 cups sliced cooked chicken

1. In a large saucepan, cook pasta in boiling water for 6 minutes.

2. Add snap peas. Return to boil. Cook 4–5 minutes, or until pasta is tender.

3. Drain pasta mixture.

4. Stir in sauce and chicken. Heat over medium heat for a few minutes, just until chicken is heated through. Stir frequently so the penne doesn't stick and scorch.

Variation:

Add a couple handfuls of fresh spinach or frozen peas when you stir in the sauce.

Chicken Cordon Bleu Reinvented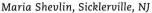

Maria Shevlin, Sicklerville, NJ

Makes 4 servings

Prep. Time: 8 minutes ⚬ *Cooking Time: 20–22 minutes*

1 Tbsp. olive oil

½ onion, diced fine

3 cloves garlic, minced

3 ribs celery, diced fine

2 chicken breasts, cubed into bite-sized pieces

2 cups deli ham, cubed

Salt, pepper, and garlic powder to taste

2 Tbsp. Dijon mustard

2 Tbsp. spicy brown mustard

1 Tbsp. cream cheese

3 Tbsp. heavy whipping cream

1 Tbsp. dried chives

1 cup shredded Swiss cheese

1. In a pan, heat the oil and add the onion, garlic, celery, and chicken. Sauté for about 10–12 minutes.

2. Add in ham, salt, pepper, and garlic powder, and stir to mix well.

3. Add in the mustards, cream cheese, heavy whipping cream, and chives. Mix well. Cook for an additional 10 minutes.

4. Serve plated with the Swiss cheese over the top.

Tip:

Optionally, you can make this in an oven-safe pan; add the Swiss cheese when it's done cooking, then place the pan under the broiler for a few minutes to brown the cheese.

Serving suggestion:

This goes well with steamed broccoli.

Sweet & Sour Chicken

Maria Shevlin, Sicklerville, NJ

Makes 4 servings

Prep. Time: 5–8 minutes ⚬ *Cooking Time: 20 minutes*

I lb. boneless skinless chicken breast, cubed

I medium onion, chopped

I cup cubed bell peppers, any color

I Tbsp. avocado oil

¼ cup water chestnuts

Green onion, sliced, *optional*

Sauce:

2 Tbsp. ketchup

½ cup white vinegar

¼ cup sweetener of your choice

I Tbsp. coconut aminos or soy sauce

I tsp. garlic powder

⅛ cup pineapple juice

¼ tsp. pink salt

¼ tsp. black pepper

½ tsp. paprika

½ tsp. ground ginger

½ tsp. ginger paste

1. Add the chicken to your air fryer set on 400°F for approximately 8 minutes, stop halfway, and turn over or shake it up to turn chicken.

2. Meanwhile cook onion and bell pepper until al dente in a pan with avocado oil.

3. Add the chicken to the pan with the veggies, along with the water chestnuts, remaining seasonings, and all the sauce ingredients. Mix well. Cook approximately 5–10 minutes, stirring to coat everything evenly.

4. Serve with the green onion if desired.

Chicken Broccoli Lo Mein

STOVETOP

Pamela Pierce, Annville, PA

Makes 4–6 servings

Prep. Time: 10 minutes Cooking Time: 15 minutes

¼ cup peanut butter

¼ cup soy sauce

1½ Tbsp. brown sugar

1 Tbsp. fresh lemon juice

⅓ cup hot water

2 cloves garlic, minced

2 Tbsp. oil

1 lb. uncooked boneless, skinless chicken breasts, cubed

1 medium bunch broccoli, cut in bite-sized pieces

½ lb. fettucine or lo mein noodles, cooked and set aside

1. In a jar with a tight lid, mix peanut butter, soy sauce, brown sugar, lemon juice, hot water, and garlic. Shake well until blended.

2. In skillet, stir-fry chicken in oil for 5–6 minutes. Add broccoli. Cook an additional 3–4 minutes.

3. Add sauce to skillet. Stir in noodles. Cook 2 more minutes and then serve.

Chicken and Quinoa Veggie Bowl

OVEN

Hope Comerford, Clinton Township, MI

Makes 4 servings

Prep. Time: 10 minutes   Baking Time: 15 minutes

½ cup quinoa

3 bunches broccolini

2 cups cherry tomatoes

½ cup sliced red onion

¼ cup olive oil, *divided*

Salt to taste

Pepper to taste

2 cups chopped rotisserie chicken meat

2 avocados, sliced, *divided*

1. Cook the quinoa according to the package directions. While it is simmering and resting, proceed with the following steps.

2. Preheat the oven to 375°F.

3. Trim 2 inches off the ends of the broccolini.

4. Between 2 baking sheets, spread out the broccolini. Arrange the cherry tomatoes and red onion around and between the broccolini.

5. Drizzle each pan of vegetables with 2 Tbsp. olive oil. Sprinkle each with the desired amount of salt and pepper.

6. Place in oven and bake for 15 minutes.

7. Divide the quinoa evenly between 4 bowls. Divide the chicken evenly between the 4 bowls.

8. When the vegetables are done, divide the vegetables evenly between the 4 bowls.

9. Top each bowl with ½ of a sliced avocado.

10. Eat and enjoy!

Egg Roll in a Bowl

Maria Shevlin, Sicklerville, NJ

Makes 6–8 servings

Prep. Time: 5–8 minutes   Cooking Time: 20–22 minutes

2 tsp. olive oil

1 lb. ground chicken sausage

2 onions, diced

6 cloves garlic, minced

1 heaping cup diced bell peppers

2 cups shredded/chopped cabbage, packed

1 cup frozen cauliflower, thawed

1 cup frozen broccoli, thawed

3 eggs, scrambled

4 green onions, chopped

1. Heat the olive oil in a pan and brown the chicken sausage with the onions and garlic.

2. Add in the peppers, cabbage, broccoli, and cauliflower and mix well. Cook an additional 10 minutes.

3. When done cooking, gently fold in the cooked eggs. Top with the green onion.

Chicken Sausage over Mashed Potatoes

Hope Comerford, Clinton Township, MI

Makes 6 servings

Prep. Time: 5–8 minutes ⚬ *Cooking Time: 20–25 minutes*

2 Tbsp. olive oil

1 large onion, sliced in half, then sliced into thin strips

2 (12-oz.) pkgs. chicken sausage (your favorite flavor)

1 red bell pepper, sliced into half rings

1 yellow bell pepper, sliced into half rings

32 oz. precooked mashed potatoes

1. Heat the olive oil in a large frying pan, then add in the onion. Cook for about 5 minutes, then add the sausages and bell peppers. Cook an additional 15–20 minutes.

2. Meanwhile, heat the precooked mashed potatoes in the microwave.

3. Serve the sausage mixture over mashed potatoes on each plate.

Serving suggestion:
Serve with a salad.

Firecracker Ground Chicken and Green Beans

Maria Shevlin, Sicklerville, NJ

Makes 4 servings

Prep. Time: 5 minutes & *Cooking Time: 15 minutes*

4 cups frozen green beans, thawed and steamed

1 cup water

1 Tbsp. avocado oil

2 lb. ground chicken, turkey, or beef

2–3 Tbsp. dried onion flakes

2–3 tsp. paprika (not smoked)

1 tsp. onion powder

1 tsp. garlic powder

½ tsp. salt

½ tsp. black pepper

1–2 heaping tsp. crushed red pepper flakes (depends on your desired spice level)

¼ cup brown sugar

¼–½ cup additional water, *optional*

1. In a pot, steam the green beans with the 1 cup of water, then set aside, covered, to keep warm.

2. Meanwhile, in a large fry pan, heat the oil and ground protein of choice, cook until half done,

3. Add in the seasonings, the green beans, and the brown sugar, and continue to cook until the ground protein is done. Add water if desired.

4. Mix well; taste and adjust seasonings.

Serving suggestion:

Serve with avocado if desired and/or over microwaveable steamed rice.

Note:

If you prefer to enjoy this without the spice, just omit the red pepper flakes.

Chicken and Broccoli Pita Sandwiches

Vonnie Oyer, Hubbard, OR

Makes 4–6 servings

Prep. Time: 15 minutes

2 cups chopped cooked chicken

2 tomatoes, chopped

1½ cups chopped raw broccoli

1 hard-cooked egg, chopped

⅓ cup cooked rice

½ cup grated cheese

1 avocado, chopped, *optional*

4 pita breads

Dressing:

2 Tbsp. honey

2 Tbsp. prepared mustard

¾ cup mayonnaise

1. Mix chicken, tomatoes, broccoli, egg, rice, cheese, and avocado together in a large bowl.

2. Mix dressing ingredients in a small bowl.

3. Pour dressing over chicken mixture and stir gently.

4. Cut pita breads in half. Fill with chicken mixture.

Mamma Ree's Sloppy Joe– Like Pulled Chicken

Maria Shevlin, Sicklerville, NJ

Makes 4 servings

Prep. Time: 5–8 minutes ❧ *Cooking Time: 15 minutes*

1 large rotisserie chicken

14½-oz. can petite diced tomatoes

⅓ cup minced onion

2 Tbsp. diced bell pepper

¾ cup spicy tomato ketchup

3 cloves garlic, minced

¼ cup chicken stock or chicken bone broth

1.31-oz. pkg. Sloppy Joe dry mix

⅛ cup brown sugar, packed

1. Pull apart chicken; set aside.

2. In a large pot or saucepan add the remaining ingredients.

3. Add the chicken back in and mix well to combine.

4. Cover and simmer 10 minutes.

Serving suggestion:
Serve on a plate or hamburger buns with a side of pickles.

Soft Chicken Tacos

Natalia Showalter, Mount Solon, VA

Makes 5–6 servings

Prep. Time: 15 minutes   *Cooking Time: 15 minutes*

1 lb. boneless, skinless chicken breasts, cubed

15-oz. can black beans, rinsed and drained

1 cup salsa

1 Tbsp. taco seasoning

6 flour tortillas, warmed

1. In nonstick skillet, cook chicken until juices run clear.

2. Add beans, salsa, and seasoning. Heat through.

3. Spoon chicken mixture down center of each tortilla.

4. Garnish with toppings of your choice.

Buffalo Chicken Meatballs

Maria Shevlin, Sicklerville, NJ

Makes 2–3 servings

Prep. Time: 5 minutes ⚬ Cooking Time: 25 minutes

Meatballs:

1 lb. ground chicken or turkey

1 Tbsp. minced onion

1 tsp. garlic powder

1 egg, beaten

1.25-oz. bag of pork rinds, ground
(I used the spicy ones)

Salt to taste

Pepper to taste

Sauce:

2 cups tomato sauce

¼–½ cup hot sauce

1 tsp. garlic powder

½ tsp. salt

½ tsp. black pepper

1 Tbsp. parsley flakes

1. Combine all meatball ingredients and roll into approximately 16–18 meatballs.

2. Cook in a nonstick pan, lightly sprayed with nonstick spray. Brown on all sides, then cook about 15 minutes, or until cooked through.

3. Mix the sauce ingredients in a pan. Add to the browned meatballs, cover, and simmer for approximately 10 minutes over low heat. Stir gently.

Loaded Rotisserie Nachos

Hope Comerford, Clinton Township, MI

Makes 6 servings

Prep. Time: 10 minutes   Baking Time: 10–12 minutes

12-oz. bag tortilla chips or strips

2 cups shredded rotisserie chicken meat

15-oz. can pinto beans, drained

½ cup sliced kalamata olives

½ cup diced onions

2 cups shredded cheddar cheese

2 cups shredded Monterey Jack cheese

⅓ cup sliced fresh jalapeños

1 avocado, diced

⅓ cup chopped fresh cilantro

1. Preheat the oven to 425°F.

2. Spread the tortilla chips out on a baking sheet.

3. Evenly spread the rotisserie chicken meat, pinto beans, kalamata olives, and diced onions over the top of the chips.

4. Sprinkle the cheese evenly over the top of all the toppings.

5. Top the cheese with the fresh jalapeño slices.

6. Bake in the oven for 10–12 minutes, or until cheese is melted.

7. Top with the avocado and cilantro.

8. Serve and enjoy!

Serving suggestion:

You can always top these loaded nachos with sour cream and fresh salsa as well, or just serve them alongside.

Barbecue Chicken Pizza

Hope Comerford, Clinton Township, MI

Makes 6 servings

Prep. Time: 10 minutes ⚘ *Baking Time: 13–15 minutes*

14-oz. premade or homemade pizza dough

½ cup sliced red onion

1 Tbsp. olive oil

1½ cups diced rotisserie chicken meat

1½ cups of your favorite barbecue sauce, *divided*

3 cups shredded mozzarella cheese

⅓ cup chopped fresh cilantro

1. Spread pizza dough on a pizza pan and bake for 5 minutes at whatever temperature the packaging suggests.

2. While the pizza dough is cooking, sauté the red onion pieces in the olive oil until they are translucent. Set aside.

3. When the pizza crust has finished its 5 minutes, remove it.

4. Spread ½ cup of the barbecue sauce over the pizza crust.

5. Toss the rotisserie chicken meat with the remaining barbecue sauce and arrange it on the pizza crust.

6. Arrange the sautéed red onion pieces on the pizza crust.

7. Sprinkle the mozzarella cheese evenly over the toppings on the pizza.

8. Bake the pizza for 8–10 minutes, or until the cheese is melted and crust is golden brown.

9. When you remove the pizza, sprinkle it with the cilantro.

10. Serve and enjoy!

Orange-Glazed Turkey Cutlets

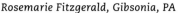

STOVETOP

Rosemarie Fitzgerald, Gibsonia, PA

Makes 4 servings

Prep. Time: 10 minutes   Cooking Time: 10 minutes

1 lb. turkey breast cutlets or slices
Salt and pepper to taste
Ground cinnamon to taste
2 tsp. oil
⅓ cup orange marmalade
⅛ tsp. ground cinnamon
⅛ tsp. ground nutmeg
⅛ tsp. ground ginger

1. Lightly sprinkle one side of cutlets with salt, pepper, and cinnamon, to taste.

2. In large nonstick skillet, over medium-high heat, sauté turkey cutlets in oil for 1–2 minutes per side, or until turkey is no longer pink in the center. Do in batches if your skillet isn't large enough to hold the cutlets all at once with space around each one.

3. Remove turkey as it finishes browning to platter and keep warm.

4. In small saucepan, over medium heat, combine marmalade, cinnamon, nutmeg, and ginger. Cook 1–2 minutes or until marmalade melts and mixture is heated through.

5. To serve, spoon marmalade sauce over cutlets.

Turkey Steaks Dijon

Christie Detamore-Hunsberger, Harrisonburg, VA

Makes 4 servings

Prep. Time: 5 minutes   Cooking Time: 15 minutes

1 lb. turkey steaks

¼ tsp. black pepper, *optional*

1½ Tbsp. butter

1 cup beef broth

1 Tbsp. cornstarch dissolved in 3 Tbsp. water

1½ Tbsp. Dijon-style mustard

⅓ cup chopped onion, *optional*

1. Sprinkle turkey steaks with pepper if you wish.

2. Heat butter in skillet.

3. Brown steaks 3 minutes per side. Remove steaks and keep warm. Drain off drippings from skillet.

4. Slowly add broth to hot pan, stirring to dissolve brown particles from bottom of pan. Stir in cornstarch dissolved in water, stirring until thickened. Stir in mustard, and onion if you wish.

5. Reduce heat to medium. Return steaks to skillet and settle into sauce. Tilt pan and spoon sauce over top of steaks.

6. Cover and simmer 2–3 minutes, or just until turkey is done.

7. Place steaks on serving platter, and spoon sauce over before serving.

Turkey Quesadillas

Tara P. Detweiler, Pennsburg, PA

Makes 8 servings

Prep. Time: 10 minutes ✂ *Cooking Time: 20 minutes*

1 lb. ground turkey

4 tsp. olive oil

1 large onion, chopped

1 red bell sweet pepper, chopped

4 cloves garlic, chopped

1 tsp. ground cumin

1 tsp. chili powder

1 tsp. dried oregano

15-oz. can tomato sauce, no salt added

15½-oz. can kidney, or black, beans, drained and rinsed

8 whole wheat flour tortillas, about 9-inch in diameter

½ cup grated cheddar cheese for topping

1. Cook ground turkey with olive oil and onion in large skillet until turkey is no longer pink.

2. Add red pepper, garlic, and all spices. Cook gently until vegetables are just tender.

3. Stir in tomato sauce and beans. Heat through.

4. Place tortillas on greased cookie sheets. Spoon turkey mixture evenly onto tortillas (approximately ¼ cup per tortilla).

5. Top each with 1 Tbsp. grated cheese.

6. Bake, uncovered, at 400°F for 15 minutes.

Thanksgiving Sliders

Maria Shevlin, Sicklerville, NJ

Makes 3–4 servings

Prep. Time: 5 minutes ❧ Cooking Time: 10–12 minutes

1 box stuffing mix
12 slider buns
14-oz. can jelly cranberry sauce
1 lb. deli turkey
2 Tbsp. butter, melted
1 tsp. parsley
½ tsp. onion powder
12 oz. jar turkey gravy
1 Tbsp. butter
1 tsp. poultry seasoning

1. Preheat oven 375°F.

2. Begin preparing the stuffing mix according to the directions on the box. While it is cooking, continue on with the following steps.

3. Slice open rolls, then add to a greased or parchment-lined baking pan.

4. Evenly add the cranberry sauce to bottom and top halves of rolls.

5. Next, add the turkey slices and stuffing.

6. Place the top halves of the buns on the bottom halves.

7. In a small bowl, mix the 2 Tbsp. of melted butter with the parsley and onion powder. Brush the tops of the buns with it.

8. Bake 10-12 minutes, or until warmed through.

9. While those are baking, warm the gravy with poultry seasoning and 1 Tbsp. of butter.

10. Plate 3–4 sliders per person, with a small bowl of gravy for dipping.

Pork

Ginger Pork Chops

Mary Fisher, Leola, PA

Makes 2 servings

Prep. Time: 10 minutes ⚘ *Cooking Time: 15 minutes*

2 (6-oz.) bone-in pork chops
1 tsp. cornstarch
2 Tbsp. low-sodium soy sauce
¼ cup honey
1 clove garlic, minced
Dash ground ginger
1 Tbsp. sliced green onion

1. Broil pork chops 3–4 inches from heat for 5–6 minutes on each side.

2. In small saucepan, combine cornstarch and soy sauce until smooth.

3. Stir in honey, garlic, and ginger.

4. Bring to a boil. Cook and stir for 1 minute, or until thickened.

5. Drizzle over cooked chops.

6. Sprinkle with green onion just before serving.

Zingy Pork Chops

Jean H. Robinson, Cinnaminson, NJ

Makes 4 servings

Prep. Time: 5 minutes 　 *Cooking Time: 20–25 minutes*

4 boneless pork loin chops
(about 1 lb.)

2 Tbsp. olive oil

½ cup apricot preserves, or orange
marmalade

Juice and zest of 1 lemon

¼ tsp. salt

½ tsp. white pepper

1 Tbsp. ground ginger, *optional*

1. Brown chops 3 minutes per side in a heavy skillet in olive oil over high heat. Do not crowd the skillet or the chops will steam in their juices rather than brown. It's better to brown them in batches.

2. Remove chops from skillet and keep warm. Reduce heat to low.

3. Add apricot preserves, lemon juice and zest, salt, pepper, and ginger if you wish, to pan drippings, as well as any juice from the pork chop plate.

4. When sauce ingredients are thoroughly blended and hot, return chops to skillet. Spoon sauce over chops. Continue heating until chops are hot but not overcooked.

Taylor's Favorite Szechuan Pork

Maria Shevlin, Sicklerville, NJ

Makes 3–4 servings

Prep. Time: 5 minutes ❧ Cooking Time: 15 minutes

2 tsp. olive oil

4 thick boneless loin chops, sliced into thin strips

1 onion, sliced

1 cup water

1–2 heaping Tbsp. chili garlic paste

2 Tbsp. sugar

3 Tbsp. tomato paste

1 tsp. coconut aminos or soy sauce

2–3 green onions, chopped, *optional*

Sesame seeds, *optional*

1. Set the Instant Pot to Sauté and heat the olive oil.

2. Sauté the pork in the Instant Pot until lightly browned.

3. Toss in the onions; stir until mixed well.

4. Add the water, chili garlic paste, sugar, and tomato paste, and simmer until thickened.

5. Stir in the coconut aminos.

6. Add as many green onions as you desire and mix well.

7. Top with the optional sesame seeds after plating.

Serving suggestion:

Serve with a side of broccoli with garlic and olive oil, and/or rice or ramen style noodles.

Note:

This recipe can easily be made on the stovetop instead of the Instant Pot.

Company Ham and Noodles

Diane Eby, Holtwood, PA

Makes 5–6 servings

Prep. Time: 5 minutes & Cooking Time: 10 minutes

6 cups water
12 oz. uncooked pasta of your choice
¼ cup chopped onion
2 Tbsp. butter
10 oz. fully cooked ham, julienned (about 2 cups)
2 tsp. flour
1 cup sour cream
Chopped fresh parsley, *optional*

1. Start water to boil in a pan. While waiting for it to come to a boil, continue on with the remaining directions. When the water does boil, cook the pasta according to the directions on the box.

2. In a skillet over medium heat, sauté onion in butter until tender.

2. Add ham. Cook and stir until heated through.

3. Sprinkle with flour and stir for 1 minute.

4. Reduce heat to low. Gradually stir in sour cream.

5. Cook and stir until thickened, about 2–3 minutes.

6. Serve over noodles. Garnish with parsley, if you wish.

Bow Tie Pasta with Peas and Bacon

J. B. Miller, Indianapolis, IN

Makes 4 servings

Prep. Time: 5 minutes ⚬ *Cooking Time: 20 minutes*

1 lb. uncooked bow tie pasta
3 strips bacon
2–3 oz. bleu cheese
2 cups frozen peas
Salt and pepper to taste

1. Cook pasta in boiling, salted water as directed on package.

2. While the pasta cooks, dice bacon and crumble cheese.

3. In a large skillet, cook bacon over medium-high heat until crisp. Remove and drain bacon, keeping 1 Tbsp. of the pan drippings.

4. When the pasta is done but before draining it, stir frozen peas into pasta cooking water. Drain well and place in large bowl.

5. Add bacon, cheese, and reserved pan drippings to pasta and peas. Toss.

6. Add salt and freshly ground pepper to taste. Mix well and serve.

Tip:

Substitute asparagus cut into bite-sized pieces for the peas!

Tortellini Carbonara

Monica Yoder, Millersburg, OH

Makes 4 servings

Prep. Time: 2 minutes ⚓ Cooking Time: 25 minutes

8 strips bacon, cooked and crumbled, or ½ cup prepared cooked and crumbled bacon

1 cup whipping cream

½ cup fresh parsley, chopped

½ cup grated Parmesan, or Romano, cheese

9-oz. pkg. cheese tortellini

1. Combine bacon, cream, parsley, and cheese in a large saucepan. Cook over low heat until hot. Stir frequently to prevent sticking and scorching.

2. Meanwhile, cook tortellini according to package directions. Drain and transfer to a serving dish.

3. Drizzle cheese sauce over tortellini and toss to coat.

Jiffy Jambalaya

Carole M. Mackie, Williamsfield, IL

Makes 6 servings

Prep. Time: 10 minutes ❧ Cooking Time: 10–15 minutes

1 onion, chopped

½ cup chopped green bell pepper

2 Tbsp. oil

1 lb. cooked kielbasa, cut into ¼-inch slices

28-oz. can diced tomatoes, undrained, or 10–12 whole tomatoes, peeled and diced

½ cup water

1 Tbsp. sugar

1 tsp. paprika

1½ tsp. fresh minced thyme

1½ tsp. fresh chopped oregano

1 small clove garlic, minced

3 drops hot pepper sauce

1½ cups uncooked instant rice

1. In skillet, sauté onion and green pepper in oil until tender.

2. Stir in sausage, tomatoes, water, sugar, and seasonings. Bring to a boil.

3. Add rice. Cover and simmer for 5 minutes, until rice is tender.

Sweet and Sour Sausage Stir-Fry

Colleen Heatwole, Burton, WI

Makes 4–6 servings

Prep. Time: 15 minutes   *Cooking Time: 15 minutes*

2–3 cups instant rice

I lb. reduced-fat kielbasa, cut into
½-inch-thick slices

½–¾ cup chopped onion

I cup shredded carrots

8-oz. can unsweetened pineapple
chunks, or tidbits

I Tbsp. cornstarch

½–I tsp. ground ginger

6 Tbsp. water

2 Tbsp. reduced-sodium soy sauce

1. Begin by preparing the Minute Rice according to the box directions. Once it is cooking, proceed with the following steps.

2. In large nonstick skillet, stir-fry sausage 3–4 minutes, or until lightly browned.

3. Add onions and carrots. Stir-fry until crisp-tender.

4. Drain pineapple, reserving juice. Add pineapple to sausage-vegetable mixture.

5. In small bowl, combine cornstarch and ginger. Stir in water, soy sauce, and reserved pineapple juice until smooth.

6. Add sauce to skillet.

7. Bring to boil. Cook, stirring continually 1–2 minutes, or until sauce is thickened.

8. Serve over rice.

Tip:

You can double everything in the recipe except the meat, and it is still excellent.

Coke Kielbasa

Shelia Heil, Lancaster, PA

Makes 3–4 servings

Prep. Time: 10 minutes   Cooking Time: 15 minutes

1 ½–2 cups uncooked instant rice
1-lb. pkg. kielbasa
12-oz. can cola
¼ cup brown sugar

1. Begin by preparing the Minute Rice according to the box directions. Once it is cooking, proceed with the following steps.

2. Slice kielbasa diagonally into ⅓-inch-thick slices.

3. Place in a medium-sized saucepan. Stir in cola and brown sugar.

4. Simmer over low heat for about 15 minutes, uncovered. Stir frequently to prevent the sauce from sticking as it thickens.

5. Serve over the rice.

Italian Subs

Susan Kasting, Jenks, OK

Makes 6 servings

Prep. Time: 15 minutes   Cooking Time: 15 minutes

6 Italian sausages

1 green bell pepper, sliced in ¼-inch strips

1 red bell pepper, sliced in ¼-inch strips

1 medium onion, sliced in ¼-inch rounds

6 hoagie rolls, split

1. Pan-fry sausages until browned on all sides.

2. In a separate pan sprayed with nonstick cooking spray, heat to medium-high heat and sauté the peppers and onions until tender-crisp.

3. Place one sausage and a generous amount of the pepper-onion mix in each hoagie roll. Serve immediately.

Healthy Sloppy Joes

Gladys M. High, Ephrata, PA

Makes 4 servings

Prep. Time: 10 minutes   Cooking Time: 20 minutes

¾ lb. 90%-lean ground pork loin

1 cup chopped onion

1 medium bell sweet pepper, chopped

1½ cups diced tomatoes, no salt added, undrained

1 medium zucchini, shredded, *optional*

1 Tbsp. chili powder

1 tsp. paprika

½ tsp. minced garlic

Pepper to taste

3 Tbsp. tomato paste

4 whole wheat hamburger buns

1. In large skillet, cook ground pork, onion, and bell pepper until meat is brown and onion is tender. Drain off drippings.

2. Stir in diced tomatoes, zucchini if you wish, chili powder, paprika, garlic, and pepper. Cover and bring to a boil. Reduce heat.

3. Add tomato paste to thicken. Simmer, uncovered, for 5 minutes.

4. Spoon mixture into buns and enjoy.

Beef & Lamb

Hoosier Lamb Chops

Willard E. Roth, Elkhart, IN

Makes 6 servings

Prep. Time: 10 minutes ❧ Cooking Time: 20 minutes

I Tbsp. oil

6 lamb chops

I onion, finely chopped

I Tbsp. balsamic vinegar

I tsp. coarsely ground black pepper

¼ cup black currant or black raspberry jam

¼ cup red wine

I Tbsp. freshly chopped mint

1. Heat oil in skillet over medium heat. Cook chops, 2 or 3 at a time, for 2 minutes per side until browned. Set aside. Reserve drippings.

2. Sauté onion for 1 minute in same skillet. Add vinegar, pepper, jam, and wine to skillet. Cook until thickened. Stir in fresh mint.

3. Return chops to skillet. Cook 2–3 minutes per side, or until just done. Adjust seasoning. Serve.

Tip:

This sauce makes a good gravy for couscous. If you want to do that, double the amounts of the sauce ingredients, and proceed according to the recipe.

Bistro Steak with Mushrooms

Gaylene Harden, Arlington, IL

Makes 4–6 servings

Prep. Time: 10 minutes ⚬ *Cooking Time: 20 minutes*

¼ tsp. pepper, *optional*

1½- to 2-lb. boneless sirloin steak, about 1½-inch thick

2 Tbsp. oil, *divided*

2 cups sliced fresh mushrooms

10¾-oz. can golden mushroom soup

½ cup dry red wine or beef broth

3 Tbsp. Worcestershire sauce, *optional*

¼ cup water

1. If you wish, rub sides of steak with ¼ tsp. pepper.

2. Heat 1 Tbsp. oil over medium-high heat in nonstick skillet. Cook steak about 5 minutes per side for medium-rare, or more, or less, depending upon how you like your steak. Transfer steak to platter and keep warm.

3. Stir-fry mushrooms in same skillet in 1 Tbsp. oil until browned.

4. Stir in soup, wine, Worcestershire sauce if you wish, and ¼ cup water. Bring to a boil. Simmer for 3 minutes. Stir occasionally.

5. Return steak and juices to skillet. Heat through.

Serving suggestion:

The steak is great served with mashed potatoes—and it offers plenty of gravy.

Sheet Pan Steak & Veggies

OVEN

Hope Comerford, Clinton Township, MI

Makes 4 servings

Prep. Time: 10 minutes   *Cooking Time: 8–10 minutes*

1½ lb. 1-inch-thick top sirloin steak

12 oz. broccolini

8 oz. cherry tomatoes, sliced in half

1 yellow bell pepper, sliced into thin strips

2 Tbsp. olive oil

Salt to taste

Pepper to taste

¼ tsp. rosemary

¼ tsp. dried thyme

¼ tsp. oregano

1. Preheat the oven to broil.

2. Spray a baking sheet with nonstick spray, then place the steak in the center, with the vegetables around it.

3. Drizzle the olive oil all over everything, making sure to coat all sides of the steak and veggies.

4. Sprinkle with the seasonings, again moving everything around to coat all sides.

5. Place under the broiler. Cook for 4–5 minutes, then flip the steaks over, turn the veggies over and cook an additional 4–5 minutes.

Quick Steak Tacos

Hope Comerford, Clinton Township, MI

Makes 6 servings

Prep. Time: 5 minutes ⚓ *Cooking Time: 10 minutes*

1 Tbsp. olive oil

8-oz. sirloin steak

2 Tbsp. steak seasoning

1 tsp. Worcestershire sauce

½ red onion, halved and sliced

6 corn tortillas

¼ cup tomatoes

¾ cup shredded Mexican blend cheese

2 Tbsp. sour cream

6 Tbsp. fresh salsa

¼ cup chopped fresh cilantro

1. Turn the Instant Pot on the Sauté function. When the pot displays "hot," add the olive oil to the pot.

2. Season the steak with the steak seasoning.

3. Add the steak to the pot along with the Worcestershire sauce.

4. Cook each side of the steak for 2–3 minutes until the steak turns brown.

5. Remove the steak from the pot and slice thinly.

6. Add the onion to the pot and cook until translucent with the remaining olive oil and steak juices.

7. Remove the onion from the pot.

8. Warm your corn tortillas, then assemble your steak, onion, tomatoes, cheese, sour cream, salsa, and cilantro on top of each.

Note:

This recipe can easily be made on the stovetop instead of the Instant Pot.

Quick and Easy Tacos

Audrey Romonosky, Austin, TX

Makes 4–6 servings

Prep. Time: 5 minutes   Cooking Time: 20 minutes

1 lb. ground beef

1 cup frozen corn

½–1 cup salsa or picante sauce, according to your taste preference

10–12 tortillas

Guacamole, *optional*

1½ cups grated cheddar cheese, *optional*

1. Brown ground beef in a skillet. Drain off drippings.

2. Add frozen corn and salsa. Cover and simmer 5–10 minutes.

3. Spoon into tortillas and garnish with guacamole and with cheese if you wish.

Tip:

Cook the corn and offer it as a topping, rather than mixing it into the filling. Then those who don't enjoy corn won't have it in their tacos, and those who do enjoy it can add it.

Cheese Steak Stuffed Bell Pepper Rings

Maria Shevlin, Sicklerville, NJ

Makes 3–4 servings

Prep. Time: 5 minutes   Cooking Time: 25 minutes

3 large red bell peppers, or any color you prefer, sliced into rings about 1-inch thick

½ medium onion, chopped fine

1 Tbsp. olive oil

3 cloves garlic, minced

1 lb. ground beef or ground chicken

1 Tbsp. yellow mustard

1 Tbsp. ketchup

2 Tbsp. cream cheese, softened

Salt to taste

Pepper to taste

1½ tsp. garlic powder

¾ cup sharp shredded cheese (or any variety)

¼ cup fresh chopped parsley, *optional*

1. Preheat the oven to 375°F.

2. Place bell pepper rings on a baking sheet and cover. When the oven is preheated, bake for about 6–7 minutes. KEEP THE OVEN ON. Remove pan from oven and uncover peppers.

2. Meanwhile, in a large skillet or fry pan, cook up the diced onion and minced garlic in the olive oil. Add in the ground beef or chicken and continue to cook until browned.

3. Add the mustard, ketchup, cream cheese, salt, pepper, and garlic powder. Cook until done and everything is incorporated well.

4. Fill the pepper rings with the above mixture, then top with the shredded cheese and some fresh chopped parsley. Place back in the oven until cheese melts, about 4–5 minutes.

Serving suggestion:
Goes well with an arugula salad.

Can't-Get-Easier Casserole

Patricia Andreas, Wausau, WI

Makes 4 servings

Prep. Time: 5–7 minutes ☙ Cooking Time: 10–15 minutes

1 lb. ground beef

1 small onion, diced

1 can tomato soup

15.25-oz. can corn, or your favorite canned vegetable, drained

8-oz. pkg. your favorite dry pasta

Shredded cheese, *optional*

1. In a large skillet, brown ground beef and diced onion. Drain off drippings if necessary.

2. Add tomato soup and drained corn to browned meat.

3. Meanwhile, cook pasta in a saucepan according to package directions until al dente (firm but not hard). Drain.

4. Add pasta to meat mixture. Stir gently and add cheese if you wish.

Tip:

Add ½ cup salsa (whatever strength you prefer) and 2 tsp. onion flakes to Step 2, for more flavor.

20-Minute Cheeseburger Rice

Peggy Clark, Burrton, KS

Makes 4 servings

Prep. Time: 5 minutes   Cooking Time: 15 minutes

1 lb. ground beef
1¾ cups water
⅔ cup ketchup
1 Tbsp. prepared mustard
2 cups uncooked instant rice
1 cup shredded cheddar cheese

1. Brown beef in a large nonstick skillet. Drain off drippings.

2. Add water, ketchup, and mustard. Stir well. Bring to a boil.

3. Stir in rice. Sprinkle with cheese. Cover.

4. Cook on low heat for 5 minutes.

Tortilla Chip Quick Dish

Cheryl Martin, Turin, NY

Makes 6 servings

Prep. Time: 13–15 minutes & *Cooking Time: 8–10 minutes*

1 lb. ground beef or turkey, browned
1 envelope taco seasoning
16-oz. can refried beans
¾ cup water
7 oz. tortilla chips
1 cup grated cheese

1. Preheat oven to 350°F.

2. Brown meat in a skillet. Drain off drippings.

3. Add taco seasoning, refried beans, and water to browned meat, then mix.

4. Place chips in a lightly greased 9 × 13-inch baking dish. Spoon bean mixture over chips.

5. Sprinkle cheese over all.

6. Bake for 8–10 minutes, or until cheese is bubbly.

Quesadilla Casserole

Lorraine Stutzman Amstutz, Akron, PA

Makes 8 servings

Prep. Time: 15 minutes ⚬ *Cooking Time: 15 minutes*

1 lb. ground beef

½ cup chopped onion

15-oz. can tomato sauce

15-oz. can black beans, drained

15-oz. can whole-kernel corn, undrained

4½-oz. can chopped green chilies

2 tsp. chili powder

1 tsp. cumin

1 tsp. minced garlic

½ tsp. oregano

½ tsp. crushed red pepper

8 corn tortillas, *divided*

2 cups shredded cheddar cheese, *divided*

1. Brown beef and onion in skillet. Drain off any drippings.

2. Add tomato sauce, beans, corn, and chilies.

3. Stir in chili powder, cumin, garlic, oregano, and red pepper.

4. Bring to boil; simmer 5 minutes.

5. Spread half of beef mixture in greased 9 × 13-inch pan.

6. Top with 4 corn tortillas, overlapping as needed.

7. Top with half remaining beef mixture and half of cheese.

8. Top with remaining tortillas and cheese.

9. Bake at 350°F for 15 minutes.

Serving suggestion:
Serve this with chopped lettuce, fresh tomatoes, and avocado, as well as sour cream and salsa as toppings, for each person to add as they wish.

Easy Meatballs

Cindy Krestynick, Glen Lyon, PA

Makes 6 servings

Prep. Time: 15 minutes   Cooking Time: 7–15 minutes

1 lb. ground beef
3 slices white bread, torn or cubed
1 small onion, chopped
4 sprigs fresh parsley, finely chopped
3 Tbsp. grated Parmesan cheese
1 egg
1 tsp. salt
¼ tsp. pepper
¾ cup water
Vegetable oil

1. Combine beef, bread pieces, onions, parsley, cheese, egg, salt, pepper, and water in a large mixing bowl until well mixed.

2. Form into 6 or 8 meatballs.

3. Brown in oil in skillet until golden brown on each side.

Serving suggestion:
Serve with spaghetti sauce in hoagie rolls, or over cooked spaghetti.

Teriyaki Burgers

Susan Kasting, Jenks, OK

Makes 4 servings

Prep. Time: 10 minutes *Cooking Time: 10 minutes*

1 lb. ground beef
2 Tbsp. soy sauce
1 Tbsp. peeled fresh ginger, grated
1 clove garlic, minced
¼ cup chopped green onions
Pinch pepper

1. Combine all ingredients in bowl.

2. Form into 4 patties.

3. Grill or broil for 10 minutes, flipping to brown both sides.

Mild Indian Curry

Vic and Christina Buckwalter, Keezletown, VA

Makes 4–6 servings

Prep. Time: 10 minutes ⚬ *Cooking Time: 15–20 minutes*

2–3 cups uncooked basmati rice

I lb. ground beef

I onion, chopped

3 cloves garlic, finely chopped

I Tbsp. freshly grated ginger

2 tsp. coriander

2 tsp. cumin

I tsp. turmeric

¼ tsp. ground cloves

¼ tsp. cayenne pepper

¾ cup tomato sauce

2 tsp. salt

2 Tbsp. sugar

¼ cup plain yogurt

Topping Options:

Grated cheeses

Chopped fresh onions

Orange sections

Sliced bananas

Chopped papaya

Chopped mango

Chopped tomatoes

Peanuts

Raisins

1. Begin by preparing the basmati rice according to the box directions. Once it is cooking, proceed with the following steps.

2. In a large skillet, brown beef, onion, and garlic together. Drain off any drippings.

3. Add ginger, coriander, cumin, turmeric, ground cloves, and cayenne pepper to beef mixture. Cook 1 minute.

4. Stir in tomato sauce, salt, and sugar. Cook 10 minutes.

5. Just before serving, blend in yogurt.

6. Serve over basmati rice.

7. Send small bowls of each topping that you choose around the table after the rice and curry have been passed.

Barbecue Sloppy Joes

STOVETOP

Winifred Paul, Scottdale, PA

Makes 5 sandwiches

Prep. Time: 10 minutes   Cooking Time: 15 minutes

¾ lb. ground beef
1 Tbsp. oil
1 tsp. lemon juice
1 Tbsp. vinegar
2 Tbsp. water
½ cup ketchup
1 tsp. brown sugar
1 tsp. finely chopped onion
⅓ cup chopped celery
1 tsp. dry mustard
5 sandwich buns

1. Brown beef in oil in skillet. Stir frequently to break up clumps and to make sure meat browns completely. Drain off drippings.

2. Make sauce by combining lemon juice, vinegar, water, ketchup, brown sugar, onion, celery, and dry mustard in saucepan.

3. Heat thoroughly, but do not cook enough to soften vegetables.

4. When beginning to simmer, combine with meat. Serve on buns.

Biscuit Tostadas

Angie Clemens, Dayton, VA

Makes 16 servings

Prep. Time: 10 minutes   ❧   Cooking Time: 15–20 minutes

1 lb. ground beef

1½ cups salsa

8-biscuit tube refrigerated large biscuits

2 cups shredded lettuce, *optional*

Sliced green onions, *optional*

2 cups shredded cheese, your choice of cheddar, Colby, or Monterey Jack

1. Preheat oven to 350°F.

2. Brown ground beef in a skillet. Drain off drippings.

3. Stir in salsa. Heat through.

4. Meanwhile, split each biscuit in half and flatten into 4-inch rounds.

5. Place biscuit halves on ungreased cookie sheet. Bake for 10–12 minutes, or until golden brown.

6. Top with meat-salsa mixture, lettuce, sliced green onions, and cheese. Serve immediately.

Reubens

Lynne Bandel, Arcadia, IN

Makes 8 servings

Prep. Time: 15 minutes   Cooking Time: 5 minutes

24-oz. unsliced loaf of rye bread

½ cup Thousand Island dressing

1 lb. cooked corned beef, or veggie corned beef, sliced thin or chipped

32-oz. can sauerkraut, drained

1 lb. Swiss cheese, thinly sliced

1. Split the loaf of bread in half horizontally.

2. Spread the cut side of each half with half the dressing.

3. Layer half the ingredients—in order—on each half of the loaf.

4. Place under broiler, about 5 inches below the heat, until cheese is melted.

5. Slice each half in 4 pieces and serve.

Creamed Dried Beef

Janet Oberholtzer, Ephrata, PA
Alica Denlinger, Lancaster, PA
Vera Martin, East Earl, PA
Beverly High, Bradford, PA
Hazel Lightcap Propst, Oxford, PA

Makes 4 servings

Prep. Time: 2–3 minutes ⚬ *Cooking Time: 15 minutes*

4 Tbsp. butter

¼ lb. thinly sliced dried beef, torn in pieces

4 Tbsp. flour

Dash of pepper, *optional*

2½ cups milk

2 Tbsp. grated sharp cheese, *optional*

1. In a medium-sized saucepan, melt butter. Stir in dried beef. Brown slightly.

2. Stir in flour and mix well. Brown over medium heat to prevent a raw flour taste. Sprinkle with pepper, if desired.

3. Continuing over medium heat, slowly add milk. Using a whisk or wooden spoon, stir continually until smooth and thickened. Sprinkle with cheese, if desired.

Serving suggestions:

Serve over toast, home fries, waffles, or pancakes for breakfast or supper. Or serve it as a topping for baked potatoes, mashed potatoes, or noodles for a main meal.

Better Than Ole Nicky's Beef Sliders

Maria Shevlin, Sicklerville, NJ

Makes 3–4 servings

Prep. Time: 4 minutes ⚬ *Cooking Time: 18–25 minutes*

14-oz. jar beef gravy

⅛ cup brine from pepperoncini peppers

4–6 pepperoncini peppers

1 tsp. dried onion flakes

⅛ tsp. black pepper

1 tsp. garlic powder

1 Tbsp. butter

1 lb. deli roast beef

12 slider buns

¼ lb. thin deli provolone cheese slices

2 Tbsp. butter, melted

1 tsp. parsley

½ tsp. onion powder

1. Preheat oven 375°F.

2. In a pot, warm the gravy with brine, pepperoncini peppers, dried onion flakes, pepper, garlic powder, and butter; about 5–7 minutes.

3. Add the deli beef and warm through an additional 3–5 minutes.

4. Meanwhile, slice the buns in half and add to a baking pan.

5. Add half the cheese slices to the bottom half of the buns, followed by the beef cooked in gravy, then the remaining cheese slices on top. Place the top half of the bun on top of the bottom half.

6. Mix the melted butter, parsley, and onion powder, then brush on the tops.

7. Bake 10–12 minutes until warmed through.

8. Plate 3–4 sliders per person with small bowl gravy for dipping.

Meatless

Lemony Quinoa and Chickpeas Bowls

Hope Comerford, Clinton Township, MI

Makes 4–6 servings

Prep. Time: 10 minutes & Cooking Time: 20 minutes

¾ cup quinoa

1½ cups water

½ cup lemon juice

¼ cup olive oil

¾ tsp. sea salt

¼ tsp. black pepper

1 tsp. garlic powder

1 tsp. onion powder

15-oz. can chickpeas, drained and rinsed

1 cup cherry tomatoes, sliced in half

¼ cup finely chopped red onion

1 cup chopped English cucumber

1 yellow bell pepper, diced

½ cup pitted kalamata olives, sliced in half

1 cup crumbled feta

1. In a pot, place the quinoa and water. Bring to a boil, then cover and let simmer for about 15 minutes, or until all the water is absorbed.

2. Meanwhile, make the dressing. In a small bowl, whisk together the lemon juice, olive oil, salt, pepper, onion powder, and garlic powder.

3. When the quinoa is done, divide it among bowls evenly. Evenly divide the chickpeas, cherry tomatoes, onion, cucumber, pepper, kalamata olives, and feta between bowls, on top of the quinoa.

4. Pour the desired amount of lemon dressing on top of each bowl, then serve.

Mary's Polenta

Mary Ladd, Bruce Township, MI

Makes 9–12 servings

Prep. Time: 10 minutes ⚹ Cooking Time: 5–7 minutes ⚹ Cooling Time: 5 minutes

12 cups water

1 tsp. garlic salt

1 tsp. parsley flakes

8 oz. ground yellow cornmeal

24 oz. spaghetti sauce

1. Bring the 12 cups of water to a boil.

2. Once boiling, add in the garlic salt and parsley. Slowly add the cornmeal, whisking as you go to break up any chunks.

3. Turn the heat down to medium and cook 5–7 minutes, or until thickness is firm and pulling away from the pan.

4. Pour the cornmeal into a glass 13 × 9-inch baking dish and let cool.

5. Cut evenly into 9–12 squares and serve with your favorite spaghetti sauce over the top.

Variations:

1. You can fry each piece of polenta in some olive oil, for an even more delicious meal!

2. Fry smaller slices of this and serve with syrup over the top as breakfast, alongside eggs, instead of potatoes.

Tip:

This does very well made ahead, and warmed up throughout the week.

Taco-Ritto

Marlene Fonken, Upland, CA

Makes 4 servings

Prep. Time: 20–25 minutes & Cooking Time: 5 minutes

1 Tbsp. + 1 tsp. vegetable oil

1½ cups broccoli florets

1 cup sliced fresh mushrooms

½ cup chopped green bell pepper

½ cup sliced onions

½ cup diced tomatoes

4 oz. shredded cheddar, or pepper jack, cheese

4 (1-oz.) flour tortillas, warmed

1. In a skillet, heat oil over medium-high heat. Add broccoli, mushrooms, green peppers, and onions. Stir-fry until tender-crisp, about 2–5 minutes.

2. Remove from heat and stir in tomatoes and cheese. Stir until cheese is partially melted.

3. Divide among the 4 tortillas. Roll up to eat!

Variation:

To add a bit more protein to this dish, use some tofu taco crumbles.

Tip:

Add some taco sauce to Step 2 if you wish.

Southwestern Pesto Pasta

Carrie Wood, Paxton, MA

Makes 4–6 servings

Prep. Time: 10 minutes ⚬ *Cooking Time: 10–12 minutes*

1 cup loosely packed cilantro leaves

1 cup loosely packed flat parsley

⅓ cup toasted pepitas (pumpkin seeds)

1 clove garlic, peeled

½ cup crumbled feta cheese

½ cup extra-virgin olive oil

Salt to taste

1 lb. spaghetti or linguine

1. Process all ingredients except pasta in a food processor until a rough paste is formed, adding additional olive oil if the paste seems too dry.

2. Cook spaghetti or linguine according to package directions. Drain.

3. Toss pesto thoroughly with hot pasta and then serve.

Creamy Crunchy Mac & Cheese

Kathy Hertzler, Lancaster, PA

Makes 6 servings

Prep. Time: 15–18 minutes   *Cooking Time: 10–12 minutes*

1 lb. uncooked macaroni

2 cups 2% milk

½ stick (4 Tbsp.) butter

3 Tbsp. flour

5 cups shredded cheddar cheese, *divided*

½ tsp. seasoned salt

½ tsp. ground black pepper

1 tsp. dry mustard

1 tsp. garlic powder, or 2 cloves garlic, minced

1 tsp. onion powder, or ¼ cup onions, chopped

¾ cup crushed cornflakes

Tip:

Don't boil the sauce after the cheese has been added. It's best to add the cheese to the sauce, stir, and remove from heat. Boiled cheese sauces usually curdle a bit or separate and don't look appetizing.

1. Cook macaroni until al dente, according to package directions, about 7 minutes. Drain well.

2. While pasta is cooking, warm milk until steamy but not boiling.

3. In another medium-sized saucepan, melt butter. Add flour, and whisk until smooth.

4. Add warm milk to butter/flour mixture. Whisk until smooth.

5. Cook, stirring constantly, on low heat for 2 minutes.

6. Add 4 cups shredded cheddar. Stir well, and then remove from heat. Set aside.

7. Stir salt, pepper, mustard, minced garlic or garlic powder, and chopped onions or onion powder into creamy sauce.

8. Place cooked macaroni in large mixing bowl.

9. Stir in cheese sauce.

10. Transfer mixture to greased 9 × 13-inch baking dish.

11. Sprinkle with cornflakes, and then remaining shredded cheddar.

12. Bake at 400°F 10–12 minutes, or until hot and bubbly.

Seafood

Maple-Glazed Salmon

Jenelle Miller, Marion, SD

Makes 6 servings

Prep. Time: 5 minutes   Cooking Time: 3 minutes

2 tsp. paprika

2 tsp. chili powder

½ tsp. ground cumin

½ tsp. brown sugar

½ tsp. kosher salt

6 (4-ounce) salmon fillets

Nonstick cooking spray

1 Tbsp. maple syrup

1 cup water

1. In a small bowl, combine the first five ingredients.

2. Rub the fillets with the seasoning mixture.

3. Spray a 7-inch round baking pan with nonstick cooking spray, and place the salmon in the pan skin-side down. Drizzle the fish with the maple syrup.

4. Pour the water into the inner pot of the Instant Pot, then place the baking pan on the trivet and carefully lower it into the pot, handles up.

5. Secure the lid and set the vent to sealing.

6. Manually set the cook time for 3 minutes on high pressure.

7. When the cooking time is over, manually release the pressure.

8. When the pin drops, remove the lid and carefully remove the trivet from the inner pot with oven mitts. Check to make sure the fillets are at 145°F.

Nutty Salmon

OVEN

Mary Seielstad, Sparks, NV

Makes 4 servings

Prep. Time: 5–10 minutes & *Baking Time: 20 minutes*

2 Tbsp. Dijon mustard
2 Tbsp. olive oil
½ cup ground pecans
1 ½ lb. salmon filets (4 6-oz. pieces)

1. In a mixing bowl, mix together mustard, oil, and pecans.

2. Spread on salmon fillets.

3. Place on an oiled baking pan.

4. Bake at 375°F for 15–18 minutes, or until fish flakes easily.

Tips:

1. You can cook this recipe on the grill. Watch closely to see that the topping doesn't burn and that you don't overcook the fish.

2. You can easily double this recipe.

Quick Salmon Patties

Dorothy VanDeest, Memphis, TN

Makes 3 servings

Prep. Time: 10 minutes   *Cooking Time: 3–4 minutes*

2 (6-oz.) cans salmon, boned, skinned, and drained

2 egg whites, or egg substitute equivalent to 1 egg

½ tsp. Worcestershire sauce

⅛ tsp. pepper

⅓ cup finely chopped onion

5 soda crackers with unsalted tops, crushed

2 tsp. olive oil

1. In a good-sized bowl, combine first six ingredients and mix well.

2. Shape into six patties.

3. In a skillet, cook patties in oil over medium heat for 1½–2 minutes.

4. Flip patties over. Cook 1½–2 minutes more, or until heated through.

Shrimp Chow Mein

Maria Shevlin, Sicklerville, NJ

Makes 6 servings

Prep. Time: 10 minutes ❧ *Cooking Time: 15–20 minutes*

1 tsp. olive oil or avocado oil

3 cloves garlic, minced

1 lb. large shrimp, peeled and deveined

1 tsp. ginger paste

¼ tsp. salt

1¼ tsp. white pepper

½ tsp. onion powder

½ tsp. garlic powder

¼ tsp. ground ginger

1 cup chicken stock

1 tsp. coconut aminos

1 medium onion, sliced thin

3 stalks celery, sliced on an angle (reserve leaves for use in dish)

¾ cup mushrooms, sliced

3 green onions, chopped

¼ cup sliced water chestnuts

1¼ cups fresh broccoli

1 Tbsp. cornstarch

1 Tbsp. cold water

1. Add the olive oil and garlic to a large skillet.

2. Add the shrimp and cook approximately 3 minutes.

3. Add the ginger paste, seasonings, stock, and coconut aminos, then mix well.

4. Toss in the onion, celery, and mushrooms. Cover and cook approximately 3–5 minutes.

5. Add in the green onion and water chestnuts; mix well. (Reserve a couple teaspoons for topping if desired.)

6. Add broccoli. Cover and cook an additional 2–3 minutes, or longer until desired tenderness is reached.

7. Stir in the celery leaves.

8. Lastly, mix the cornstarch and water, then stir it in, turn up the heat, and allow to boil to thicken up.

Serving suggestion:

Serve with steamed white or brown rice.

Shrimp Stir-Fry

Jean Binns Smith, Bellefonte, PA

Makes 4 servings

Prep. Time: 10 minutes *Cooking Time: 8–10 minutes*

1–2 cloves garlic, chopped

⅛ tsp. grated, or finely chopped, fresh ginger

1 Tbsp. olive oil

2½ cups (about ½ lb.) fresh sugar snap peas

½ cup chopped red bell sweet pepper, *optional*

12 oz. medium-sized raw shrimp, peeled and deveined

1. Sauté garlic and ginger in oil in large skillet until fragrant.

2. Stir in sugar snap peas and chopped pepper if you wish. Sauté until crisp-tender.

3. Stir in shrimp. Cook over medium heat 3–4 minutes until shrimp are just opaque in centers.

Serving suggestion:

Serve with steamed rice.

Shrimp with Ginger and Lime

STOVETOP

Joy Uhler, Richardson, TX

Makes 2–4 servings

Prep. Time: 15–20 minutes ⚬ *Cooking Time: 10 minutes*

1–2 cups uncooked instant rice

3 Tbsp. fresh lime juice

4 Tbsp. olive oil, *divided*

1 Tbsp. fresh minced ginger

1 Tbsp. brown sugar

1 tsp. grated lime zest

1 tsp. sesame seed oil

1 large clove garlic, minced

1 lb. cooked shrimp, peeled and deveined

2 Tbsp. fresh chopped cilantro

1. Begin by preparing the Minute Rice according to the box directions. Once it is cooking, proceed with the following steps.

2. In a large mixing bowl, stir together lime juice, 3 Tbsp. olive oil, ginger, brown sugar, lime zest, sesame seed oil, and garlic.

3. Stir in shrimp and mix well until covered with the marinade. Allow shrimp to marinate for 15 minutes.

4. Pour 1 Tbsp. olive oil into large skillet or wok. Spoon in shrimp mixture and stir-fry until heated through.

5. Serve over prepared rice. Sprinkle with chopped cilantro.

Creole Shrimp

Maria Shevlin, Sicklerville, NJ

Makes 4 servings

Prep. Time: 8 minutes 🐟 *Cooking Time: 18 minutes*

I tsp. olive oil

2 cloves garlic, minced or grated

½ lb. medium shrimp, peeled, deveined

½ cup chopped celery

½ cup chopped onion

4 mini bell peppers, chopped (I used red, yellow, and orange)

½ lb. medium shrimp, peeled and deveined

1½ tsp. Emeril's Original Essence All Purpose Seasoning Blend

3 slices turkey ham or regular ham, sliced and diced

1¼ cups chicken or veggie stock

I Tbsp. cornstarch

2 green onions, chopped

14-oz. bag Better Than Rice

1. Add olive oil to a large fry pan with the garlic. Cook for 1 minute in oil.

2. Add the celery, onion, and bell peppers. Cover and cook 5–6 minutes. Stir often.

3. Add the shrimp and Emeril's Essence. Stir to combine.

4. Add the ham, then stir to mix well. Cover and cook 2 minutes.

5. Mix the stock with the cornstarch, then add it to the pan.

6. Toss in the green onion. Bring to a low boil. Cover and cook 3–4 minutes, and stir to mix evenly. The shrimp will cook in the simmering sauce.

7. Warm the Better Than Rice according to the directions on the bag, then serve the Creole Shrimp over it.

Tip:

You can top with additional green onion and Essence if desired.

Cajun Shrimp

Mary Ann Potenta, Bridgewater, NJ

Makes 4–5 servings

Prep. Time: 5 minutes   *Cooking Time: 10–12 minutes*

2–2 ½ cups uncooked Minute Rice

1 ½ sticks (12 Tbsp.) butter, *divided*

½ cup chopped green onions

1 tsp. minced garlic

1 tsp. cayenne pepper

½ tsp. white pepper

½ tsp. black pepper

¼ tsp. dry mustard

½ tsp. salt

1 tsp. Tabasco sauce

2 lb. shrimp, peeled and cleaned

1. Begin by preparing the Minute Rice according to the box directions. Once it is cooking, proceed with the following steps.

2. Melt 1 stick of butter in large skillet. Add onions and garlic and sauté till clear, but not brown, about 1 minute.

3. Add peppers, mustard, and salt. Cook and stir for 3 minutes.

4. Mix in half-stick of butter and Tabasco sauce until blended.

5. Add shrimp. Cook just until pink. Do not overcook.

6. Serve over cooked rice.

Note:

This is hot! You can tone things down by reducing the amounts of the peppers and the Tabasco sauce.

Shrimp in Vodka Sauce

Maria Shevlin, Sicklerville, NJ

Makes 3–4 servings

Prep. Time: 5 minutes ❧ Cooking Time: 10 minutes

1 Tbsp. olive oil

½ medium onion, chopped fine

2–3 cloves garlic, minced

24-oz. jar favorite spaghetti sauce or homemade

1 tsp. salt

⅛–¼ tsp. pepper

Pinch or two red pepper flakes

¾–1 cup vodka

2 Tbsp. butter

¼ cup heavy whipping cream or half-and-half

¼ cup fresh Parmesan cheese

1 lb. shrimp, peeled and deveined

1. Add the olive oil in pan with the finely chopped onion and minced garlic. Cook until al dente.

2. Add in your favorite homemade or jar spaghetti sauce, salt, pepper, and red pepper flakes. Simmer until warmed through. If you prefer a smooth sauce, blend it now.

3. Put the blended sauce back in the pan and add the vodka. Simmer for 2–3 minutes.

4. Add the butter, cream, and Parmesan cheese. Stir well.

5. Add the shrimp and cook about 3–4 minutes.

6. Taste to adjust seasonings, then serve.

Variation:

You can use precooked shredded chicken instead of shrimp if you prefer.

Shrimp Primavera

Elaine Rineer, Lancaster, PA

Makes 4 servings

Prep. Time: 20 minutes ❧ *Cooking Time: 10 minutes*

1 Tbsp. + 1 tsp. vegetable or olive oil
1½ cups chopped broccoli
½ cup thinly sliced carrots
1 cup sliced mushrooms
2 cloves garlic, minced
1 cup chicken broth
1 Tbsp. cornstarch
1 lb. shrimp, peeled and deveined
2 Tbsp. grated Parmesan cheese
2 Tbsp. parsley

1. In large skillet or wok, sauté broccoli and carrots in oil. Stir-fry until carrots are crisp-tender.

2. Stir in mushrooms and garlic. Stir-fry 1 minute.

3. In a small bowl, whisk together broth and cornstarch. Pour over vegetables.

4. Add shrimp. Cook until shrimp turns pink and sauce thickens.

5. Stir in remaining ingredients.

Shrimp & Zucchini Sauté

Maria Shevlin, Sicklerville, NJ

Makes 3–4 servings

Prep. Time: 10 minutes ❧ Cooking Time: 20 minutes

¼ cup water

1 Tbsp. olive oil

2 carrots, quartered, then sliced into half-inch chunks

3 ribs celery, sliced lengthwise then cut into half-inch chunks

3 cloves garlic, chopped

1 small red onion, chopped

1 small yellow onion, chopped

8 oz. mushrooms, sliced

2 medium zucchini, quartered, then sliced into half-inch chunks

1 lb. raw medium shrimp, peeled and deveined

Chopped green onions, for garnish

Fresh chopped parsley, for garnish

Sauce:

3-5 Tbsp. sweet chili sauce

1 Tbsp. sambal oelek

3–7 Tbsp. water

1 Tbsp. tamari or soy sauce

½ tsp. black pepper

½ tsp. salt

¾ tsp. garlic powder

1. Add the water and oil into a large fry pan; toss in the carrots and celery. Cover and steam for about 4 minutes over medium low heat.

2. Meanwhile, mix the sauce ingredients, then set aside.

3. When you're done steaming the carrots and celery, add in the garlic, onions, and mushrooms; stir. Cook for approximately 5–6 minutes, stirring often.

4. Toss in the zucchini and mix well to combine. Cook 1–2 minutes.

5. Add the sauce along with the shrimp. Mix well. Cover and cook for another 3–5 minutes.

6. Garnish with green onion, fresh parsley, and/or more sambal oelek.

Mamma Ree's Faux Cioppino

Maria Shevlin, Sicklerville, NJ

Makes 4 servings

Prep. Time: 10 minutes ⚜ Cooking Time: 15 minutes

1 Tbsp. olive oil

3–4 cloves garlic, minced

½ cup sliced carrots, cut in half

½ cup sliced celery

½ cup sliced onions

½ cup finely chopped cauliflower

1½ cups tomato sauce

½ cup water

Salt to taste

Pepper to taste

3 tsp. parsley flakes

1 tsp. garlic powder

1 tsp. onion powder

1 tsp. Kinder's Red Garlic (if this is unavailable add dried minced garlic and red pepper flakes)

10–20 large shrimp, shells removed and sliced in half lengthwise

1 cup half-and-half

1. Set the Instant Pot to Sauté and add the oil. When the oil is heated, add the garlic, carrots, celery, onion, and cauliflower. Sauté until al dente and keep stirring.

2. Add the tomato sauce, water, and seasonings.

3. Simmer for 1–2 minutes over low heat.

4. Place the raw shrimp into the Instant Pot. Stir. Simmer for approximately 3–4 minutes, then add the half-and-half.

Variation:

1. You can add 1/2 cup of green beans and/or diced zucchini in addition to the veggies listed above.

2. You can also add half the amount of shrimp and replace with some small scallops as well.

3. Swap the water for a dry white wine for a more authentic cioppino.

Note:

This recipe can easily be made on the stovetop instead of the Instant Pot.

Scallops in Wine Sauce

Doris M. Zipp, Germantown, NY

Makes 2–4 servings

Prep. Time: 10 minutes   *Cooking Time: 10 minutes*

1 stick (8 Tbsp.) butter
1 lb. scallops
2 Tbsp. flour
½ cup dry white wine
Fresh parsley

1. Melt butter in skillet.

2. Add scallops and sauté until barely cooked.

3. Sprinkle flour over scallops. Stir until flour is moistened. Add wine. Stir and simmer just until a creamy sauce appears. Be careful not to overcook the scallops.

4. Garnish with parsley.

Tip:

This makes a great sauce and works well served with spaghetti.

Crab Imperial

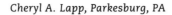

STOVETOP

Cheryl A. Lapp, Parkesburg, PA

Makes 4–6 servings

Prep. Time: 5 minutes ⚶ *Cooking Time: 20 minutes*

6 cups water
12 oz. pasta of your choice
1 lb. crabmeat
3 Tbsp. butter
2 cloves garlic, chopped fine
¼ tsp. onion powder
16-oz. jar Alfredo sauce

1. Set the water to boil. Meanwhile, proceed with the following steps. Once the water is boiling, prepare the pasta according to the package directions.

2. Cut crabmeat into small pieces.

3. Melt butter in a large skillet. Sauté crab with garlic and onion powder for 10 minutes, or until meat is hot and garlic is softened.

4. Add Alfredo sauce. Simmer over low heat another 10 minutes, stirring frequently. (Thin with ½ cup milk if the sauce seems too thick.)

5. Serve over freshly cooked noodles.

Crab Pizza

Sharon Easter, Yuba City, CA

Makes 6–8 servings

Prep. Time: 10 minutes ⚶ *Cooking Time: 13–15 minutes*

½ stick (4 Tbsp.) butter
6 green onions, sliced thin
8-oz. pkg. cream cheese, cubed
½ lb. flaked crabmeat
Prepared pizza crust

1. Melt butter in a large skillet. Add onions and cook until onions soften.

2. Toss cubed cream cheese into skillet. Heat until bubbly and melted, stirring frequently to prevent scorching.

3. Break up crab with a fork. Stir into creamy sauce in skillet. Continue heating over low heat until crab is also hot.

4. Meanwhile, heat a large pizza crust on a baking sheet in a 400°F oven for 5 minutes. Remove crust from oven.

5. Turn oven to 450°F. Spoon crab mixture onto crust. Place pizza in oven and bake 8 minutes.

Metric Equivalent Measurements

If you're accustomed to using metric measurements, I don't want you to be inconvenienced by the imperial measurements I use in this book.

Use this handy chart, too, to figure out the size of the slow cooker you'll need for each recipe.

Weight (Dry Ingredients)

1 oz		30 g
4 oz	¼ lb	120 g
8 oz	½ lb	240 g
12 oz	¾ lb	360 g
16 oz	1 lb	480 g
32 oz	2 lb	960 g

Slow Cooker Sizes

1-quart	0.96 l
2-quart	1.92 l
3-quart	2.88 l
4-quart	3.84 l
5-quart	4.80 l
6-quart	5.76 l
7-quart	6.72 l
8-quart	7.68 l

Volume (Liquid Ingredients)

½ tsp.		2 ml
1 tsp.		5 ml
1 Tbsp.	½ fl oz	15 ml
2 Tbsp.	1 fl oz	30 ml
¼ cup	2 fl oz	60 ml
⅓ cup	3 fl oz	80 ml
½ cup	4 fl oz	120 ml
⅔ cup	5 fl oz	160 ml
¾ cup	6 fl oz	180 ml
1 cup	8 fl oz	240 ml
1 pt	16 fl oz	480 ml
1 qt	32 fl oz	960 ml

Length

¼ in	6 mm
½ in	13 mm
¾ in	19 mm
1 in	25 mm
6 in	15 cm
12 in	30 cm

Index

About the Author

Hope Comerford is a mom, wife, elementary music teacher, blogger, recipe developer, public speaker, Young Living Essential Oils essential oil enthusiast/educator, and published author. In 2013, she was diagnosed with a severe gluten intolerance and since then has spent many hours creating easy, practical, and delicious gluten-free recipes that can be enjoyed by both those who are affected by gluten and those who are not.

Growing up, Hope spent many hours in the kitchen with her Meme (grandmother), and her love for cooking grew from there. While working on her master's degree when her daughter was young, Hope turned to her slow cookers for some salvation and sanity. It was from there she began truly experimenting with recipes and quickly learned she had the ability to get a little more creative in the kitchen and develop her own recipes.

In 2010, Hope started her blog, *A Busy Mom's Slow Cooker Adventures*, to simply share the recipes she was making with her family and friends. She never imagined people all over the world would begin visiting her page and sharing her recipes with others as well. In 2013, Hope self-published her first cookbook, *Slow Cooker Recipes 10 Ingredients or Less and Gluten-Free*, and then later wrote *The Gluten-Free Slow Cooker*.

Hope became the new brand ambassador and author of Fix-It and Forget-It in mid-2016. Since then, she has brought her excitement and creativeness to the Fix-It and Forget-It brand. Through Fix-It and Forget-It, she has written *Welcome Home 5-Ingredient Cookbook*, *Welcome Home Pies, Crisps, and Crumbles*, *Welcome Home Super Simple Entertaining*, *Fix-It and Forget-It Instant Pot Cookbook*, *Fix-It and Forget-It Freezer Meals*, *Fix-It and Forget-It Mediterranean Diet*, *The All-American Rotisserie Chicken Dinner*, and many more.

Hope lives in the city of Clinton Township, Michigan, near Metro Detroit. She has been happily married to her husband and best friend, Justin, since 2008. Together they have two children, Ella and Gavin, who are her motivation, inspiration, and heart. In her spare time, Hope enjoys traveling, singing, cooking, reading books, spending time with friends and family, and relaxing.